Contents

Answers

Published by CGP

ISBN: 978 1 78294 801 8

Pages 4-6 contain public sector information licensed under the Open Government Licence v3.0.
http://www.nationalarchives.gov.uk/doc/open-government-licence/version/3/

www.cgpbooks.co.uk
Printed by Elanders Ltd, Newcastle upon Tyne.
Clipart from Corel®
Cover image: © iStock.com/FrankRamspott

Text, design, layout and original illustrations © Coordination Group Publications Ltd. (CGP) 2017

About This Book

This is the matching answer book to our Maths for Key Stage 2 Year 4 Textbook.

Here you'll find a Programme of Study mapping, showing where each Year 4 requirement is covered in the Textbook. This makes it easy for you to find the pages in the Textbook you need for your lesson.

There is also a Scheme of Work which suggests the order you might want your pupils to work through the book during the school year. This uses 11-week terms so that additional weeks in each term can be used for assessment or other activities.

Finally, there are answers to every question in the Textbook.

About The Textbook

The Textbook is split into seven sections, with each one covering a different area of the Year 4 Programme of Study. These sections are:

- Section 1 — Number and Place Value
- Section 2 — Addition and Subtraction
- Section 3 — Multiplication and Division
- Section 4 — Fractions and Decimals
- Section 5 — Measurement
- Section 6 — Geometry
- Section 7 — Statistics

Within each section, all of the statutory requirements from the corresponding Programme of Study area (as well as the important non-statutory requirements) are covered. Many of the requirements are covered across several pages. This is done so that every part of each requirement is covered in depth, and the most important topics can be revisited in multiple lessons.

Topic Pages

The main topic pages start with one to three examples. These are to give pupils a brief visual reminder of how to approach some of the questions.

The questions are split into three differentiated Sets which can be assigned to pupils depending on their ability.

- Set A is for pupils working towards the expected level for Year 4.
- Set B is for pupils working at the expected level for Year 4.
- Set C is for pupils working above the expected level for Year 4.

At the end of each topic, there is a learning objective summarising the Programme of Study requirements covered in that topic. There are tick boxes here for pupils to show how confident they feel with the topic.

Review Pages

After every few topics, there is a Review page with more questions on those topics. The questions cover the full range of difficulty from the main topic pages, but are not split into differentiated Sets, so every pupil can try all the questions.

The Review pages are really useful for recapping and summarising several topics within one lesson.

Challenge Pages

At the end of each section, there are Challenge pages. These have a different style to the rest of the book — the questions test pupils' deeper understanding of the maths topics in the section. Pupils might have to investigate something, talk to a friend about a problem, or play a game. Like the review pages, the questions are not differentiated.

Answers are provided for Challenges where possible, but are not included for open-ended tasks and games.

Online Resources

On our website, you can access free printable resources that can be used with different questions throughout the book. The resources contain things such as blank clock faces, rulers and number lines, which will save pupils having to copy them out.

To access these resources, go to:
www.cgpbooks.co.uk/KS2MathsResources

Programme of Study Mapping

A mapping from the Year 4 Programme of Study to the pages of our Maths for Key Stage 2 Year 4 Textbook is given on the next three pages. As well as all of the statutory points from the Programme of Study, some important non-statutory points have also been included — these are marked with an asterisk*.

Number and Place Value

count in multiples of 6, 7, 9, 25 and 1000	4, 5
find 1000 more or less than a given number	6
count backwards through zero to include negative numbers	7
recognise the place value of each digit in a four-digit number (thousands, hundreds, tens, and ones)	2
order and compare numbers beyond 1000	9
identify, represent and estimate numbers using different representations	3
round any number to the nearest 10, 100 or 1000	10, 11
solve number and practical problems that involve all of the above and with increasingly large positive numbers	12, 13
read Roman numerals to 100 (I to C) and know that over time, the numeral system changed to include the concept of zero and place value	17, 18
*extend knowledge of the number system to include the decimal numbers and fractions that have been met so far	15, 16
Number and place value review pages	*8, 14, 19*
Number and place value challenges	*20-22*

Addition and Subtraction

add and subtract numbers with up to 4 digits using the formal written methods of columnar addition and subtraction where appropriate	29-32
estimate and use inverse operations to check answers to a calculation	34, 35
solve addition and subtraction two-step problems in contexts, deciding which operations and methods to use and why	36-39
*continue to practise mental methods of addition and subtraction with increasingly large numbers to aid fluency	23-27
Addition and subtraction review pages	*28, 33, 40*
Addition and subtraction challenges	*41-43*

Multiplication and Division

recall multiplication and division facts for multiplication tables up to 12 × 12	44-49, 55
use place value, known and derived facts to multiply and divide mentally, including: multiplying by 0 and 1; dividing by 1; multiplying together three numbers	52-54, 56
recognise and use factor pairs and commutativity in mental calculations	51
multiply two-digit and three-digit numbers by a one-digit number using formal written layout	58-60
solve problems involving multiplying and adding, including using the distributive law to multiply two digit numbers by one digit, integer scaling problems and harder correspondence problems such as n objects are connected to m objects	63-66
*practise to become fluent in the formal written method of short division with exact answers	61, 62
Multiplication and division review pages	*50, 57, 67*
Multiplication and division challenges	*68-70*

Fractions (including decimals)

recognise and show, using diagrams, families of common equivalent fractions	71, 72
count up and down in hundredths; recognise that hundredths arise when dividing an object by one hundred and dividing tenths by ten	73
solve problems involving increasingly harder fractions to calculate quantities, and fractions to divide quantities, including non-unit fractions where the answer is a whole number	76, 77
add and subtract fractions with the same denominator	74, 75
recognise and write decimal equivalents of any number of tenths or hundredths	79, 80
recognise and write decimal equivalents to $\frac{1}{4}$, $\frac{1}{2}$, $\frac{3}{4}$	81
find the effect of dividing a one- or two-digit number by 10 and 100, identifying the value of the digits in the answer as ones, tenths and hundredths	82
round decimals with one decimal place to the nearest whole number	85
compare numbers with the same number of decimal places up to two decimal places	86
solve simple measure and money problems involving fractions and decimals to two decimal places	87, 88
*practise counting using simple fractions and decimals, both forwards and backwards	73, 84
Fractions and decimals review pages	*78, 83, 89*
Fractions and decimals challenges	*90-92*

Programme of Study Mapping

Measurement

Geometry

Statistics

Scheme of Work

This Scheme of Work can be used alongside the Year 4 Textbook to cover the Year 4 Programme of Study in full. Each term is divided into 11 weeks, with suggested topics from the Textbook for each week.

Term 1 — Autumn

Scheme of Work

Term 2 — Spring

Scheme of Work

Term 3 — Summer

Week	Topic	Page
1	2D Shapes	121
	Triangles	122, 123
	Quadrilaterals	124, 125
2	Angles	126, 127
	Lines of Symmetry	128, 129
	Geometry — Review 1	*130*
3	Time — 1	110
	Time — 2	111
	Clocks	112, 113
4	Solving Problems with Time — 1	114, 115
	Solving Problems with Time — 2	116
	Measurement — Review 4	*117*
5	Perimeter	99, 100
	Area — 1	101
	Area — 2	102
6	Perimeter and Area	103
	Measurement — Review 2	*104*
	Measurement — Challenges	*118-120*
7	Reflection	131, 132
	Coordinates	133
	Translation	134
8	Plotting Points	135
	Drawing Shapes	136
	Geometry — Review 2	*137*
	Geometry — Challenges	*138-140*
9	Tables	141, 142
	Bar Charts	143, 144
	Solving Problems with Tables	150, 151
	Solving Problems with Bar Charts	152, 153
10	Pictograms	145, 146
	Time Graphs	147, 148
	Statistics — Review 1	*149*
11	Solving Problems with Pictograms	154, 155
	Solving Problems with Time Graphs	156, 157
	Statistics — Review 2	*158*
	Statistics — Challenges	*159, 160*

Section 1 — Number and Place Value

Page 2: Place Value

Set A

1. 1 thousand or 1000
2. 3 hundreds or 300
3. 5 ones or 5
4. 9 tens or 90
5. 8 thousands or 8000
6. 7 hundreds or 700
7. 3 hundreds or 300
8. 2
9. 9
10. 4
11. 8
12. 2 hundreds or 200
13. 8 ones or 8
14. 5 thousands or 5000
15. 2586

Set B

1. 1 thousand or 1000
2. 6 ones or 6
3. 9 thousands or 9000
4. 8 tens or 80
5. 3 hundreds or 300
6. 4 ones or 4
7. 7 hundreds or 700
8. 2
9. 7
10. 6
11. 2
12. 9432
13. 3 tens or 30
14. 4321
15. 3 hundreds or 300

Set C

1. 8 thousands or 8000
2. 4 tens or 40
3. 5 tens or 50
4. 9 ones or 9
5. 4 thousands or 4000
6. 9 tens or 90
7. 3 hundreds or 300
8. 5937
9. 4625
10. 9870
11. 8027
12. 9321
13. 1239
14. 1329, 1923, 3129, 3921, 9123, 9321
15. 2391, 2931, 3291, 3921, 9231, 9321

Set B

1. three thousand, four hundred
2. two thousand, one hundred and seventy
3. four thousand, two hundred and twenty
4. eight thousand, two hundred and ninety-three
5. one thousand, seven hundred and ninety-six
6. five thousand and eighty-nine
7. six thousand, six hundred and eight
8. ninety
9. five
10. eighty
11. five
12. true
13. false
14. false
15. false

Set C

1. eight thousand, nine hundred and forty-three
2. two thousand, nine hundred and twenty-five
3. five thousand, two hundred and twenty
4. seven thousand, nine hundred and eight
5. three thousand and fifty-six
6. nine thousand and nineteen
7. one thousand and ten
8. 9, eight
9. 2, hundred, six
10. 1, thousand
11. 0, thousand
12. eight thousand, five hundred and nine
13. five thousand, nine hundred and eight
14. nine thousand, eight hundred and five
15. five thousand, eight hundred and nine

Page 3: Writing Numbers

Set A

1. seven hundred
2. eight hundred and twenty-three
3. two thousand
4. six thousand, seven hundred
5. four thousand, nine hundred
6. nine thousand, one hundred and twenty
7. five thousand, five hundred and ninety-two
8. 3000
9. 781
10. 1926
11. 6585
12. 5890
13. two thousand
14. 7500
15. 2634
16. 8845
17. five thousand, nine hundred and twenty-five

Page 4: Counting in Multiples — 1

Set A

1. 7
2. 12
3. 27
4. 58
5. 49
6. 61
7. 6
8. 2
9. 4
10. 5
11. 2
12. 3
13. 2
14. 2
15. 1
16. 14
17. 2
18. 6

Set B

1. 102
2. 99
3. 96
4. 14
5. 24
6. 12
7. 1
8. 3
9. 5
10. 4
11. 1
12. 5
13. 3
14. 2
15. 3
16. 39
17. 58
18. 54

Set C

1. 1920
2. 1939
3. 1926
4. 128
5. 257
6. 12
7. 26
8. 98
9. 2
10. 7
11. 6
12. 7
13. 6
14. 9
15. 7

Page 5: Counting in Multiples — 2

Set A

1.	2075	**7.**	4	**13.**	4
2.	3000	**8.**	5	**14.**	5
3.	2100	**9.**	2	**15.**	9
4.	1170	**10.**	2	**16.**	6
5.	1550	**11.**	1	**17.**	5
6.	1300	**12.**	4	**18.**	2

Set B

1.	1690	**7.**	25	**12.**	3
2.	6290	**8.**	1000	**13.**	1
3.	1340	**9.**	25	**14.**	2
4.	2025	**10.**	10	**15.**	10
5.	2075	**11.**	5	**16.**	5
6.	2185				

Set C

1.	4163	**7.**	8750	**12.**	1000
2.	4623	**8.**	3870	**13.**	100
3.	4173	**9.**	3550	**14.**	100
4.	8330	**10.**	2750	**15.**	25
5.	2650	**11.**	3800	**16.**	10
6.	21				

Page 6: Counting 1000 Up and Down

Set A

1.	2200
2.	8200
3.	6900
4.	1020
5.	5350
6.	2408
7.	1764
8.	8926
9.	5000, 7000
10.	8920, 9920
11.	5828, 8828
12.	1200, 2200

13.

1090	—	2090
3852	—	8080
9080	—	4852
6002	—	7002
3789	——	4789

Set B

1.	1500	**9.**	eight thousand
2.	2862	**10.**	two thousand, two hundred
3.	7124	**11.**	eight thousand and fifty
4.	5288	**12.**	1000
5.	3236	**13.**	2000
6.	4445	**14.**	4025
7.	6130	**15.**	4940
8.	eight thousand		

Set C

1.	8764	**7.**	2405
2.	1573	**8.**	9076
3.	5512	**9.**	9076
4.	7008	**10.**	5420 − 3000 + 7000
5.	1016	**11.**	1782, 5782, 6782
6.	620		

Page 7: Negative Numbers

Set A

1.	−2
2.	−6
3.	−12
4.	−3
5.	−2
6.	−7

7.

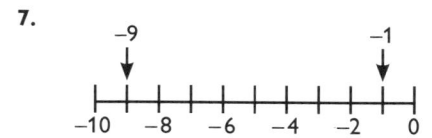

8-9.

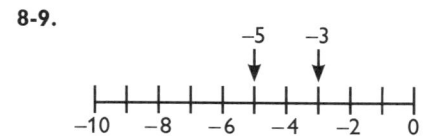

10.	less
11.	more
12.	2
13.	3
14.	4

Set B

1.	−2
2.	−7
3.	−15
4.	−4
5.	−5
6.	−2

7-8.

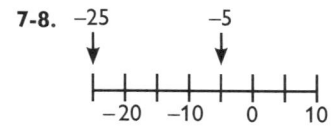

9.	8
10.	3
11.	6
12.	Lee's number is −5 and Mark's number is 3
13.	3
14.	4

Set C

1.	8
2.	4
3.	1
4.	−15
5.	−10
6.	2
7.	4

8-9.

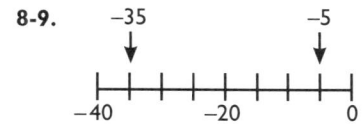

10.	−3
11.	−6
12.	−25
13.	−25
14.	−34
15.	−35
16.	−108

Page 8: Number and Place Value — Review 1

1. 1 hundred or 100
2. 7 tens or 70
3. 9 tens or 90
4. 1 thousand or 1000
5. 4 tens or 40
6. 6 thousands or 6000
7. 2 hundreds or 200
8. 1 one or 1
9. 981, 189
10. 8731, 1378
11. 8642, 2468
12. 8321, 1238
13. 9633, 3369
14. 9877, 7789
15. one hundred and fifty
16. two thousand, seven hundred
17. one thousand, nine hundred and fifty-two
18. three thousand, six hundred and seventy-eight
19. nine thousand and twelve
20. five thousand and seven
21. 200
22. 9000
23. 6300
24. 3256
25. 1399
26. 5411
27. 8028
28. 4072
29. 112
30. 128
31. 145
32. 40
33. 44
34. 19
35. 3
36. 10
37. 2
38. 6
39. 5
40. 5
41. 5025
42. 5300
43. 5050
44. 4600
45. 4880
46. 4800
47. 12
48. 9
49. 6
50. 5
51. 4897
52. 1645
53. 9810
54. 919
55. 3000
56. 4624
57. 6810
58. 3629
59. see below
60. −1
61. −5
62. −3
63. −15
64. −95
65. −45
66. −4
67. −9
68. −1
69. −4
70. −8
71. −15

59.
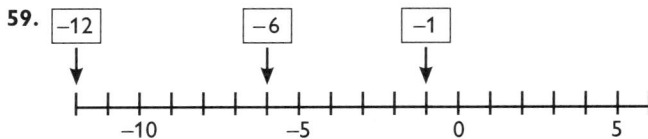

Page 9: Ordering Numbers

Set A

1. 2074
2. 1568
3. <
4. <
5. bigger
6. smaller
7. bigger
8. smaller
9. smaller
10. bigger
11. 3082, 3145, 4956
12. 8720, 8210, 7095
13. four (1000, 1001, 1002 and 1003)

Set B

1. 9890
2. 1486
3. 9243
4. 2786
5. 5586
6. 3828
7. 8055
8. 2186, 2420, 2516, 3287
9. 2
10. 1555
11. 3560
12. 5402
13. 2349

Set C

1. >
2. >
3. <
4. <
5. >
6. >
7. >
8. £7812
9. No — £7812 and £7818 are bigger than £7810
10. 3165
11. 8104
12. 6203
13. 1006
14. 9
15. 0

Page 10: Rounding — 1

Set A

1. 20
2. 820
3. 310
4. 120
5. 2730
6. 1690
7. 600

8-11.
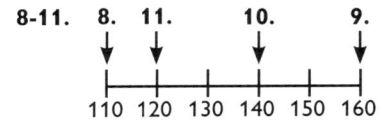

12. 78
13. 35, 36, 37, 38, 39, 40, 41, 42, 43, 44
14. 395, 396, 397, 398, 399, 400, 401, 402, 403, 404

Set B

1. 10 cm
2. 330 cm
3. 490 cm
4. 1230 cm
5. 2100 cm
6. 5200 cm
7. 7400 cm
8. 40
9. 250
10. 790
11. 1870
12. 3510
13. 19
14. 112
15. 3217

Set C

1. 990 g
2. 8010 g
3. 4300 g
4. 8250 g
5. 1390 g
6. 2000 g
7. 8670 g
8. one hundred and thirty
9. nine hundred and ninety
10. six thousand, one hundred and sixty
11. nine thousand, seven hundred and thirty
12. one thousand
13. 164
14. 2054
15. 1695, 1696, 1697, 1698, 1699, 1700, 1701, 1702, 1703, 1704

Page 11: Rounding — 2

Set A

1. 400
2. 900
3. 100
4. 3000
5. 5000
6. 1000

7.

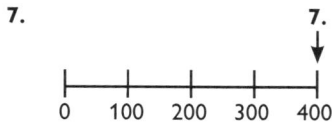

8. 1000
9. 100
10. 9000 km
11. 8000 km
12. 7000 km
13. 5000 km
14. 2000 km

Set B

1. 800 ml
2. 200 ml
3. 1100 ml
4. 7100 ml
5. 2700 ml
6. 8100 ml
7. 6900 ml

8-11.

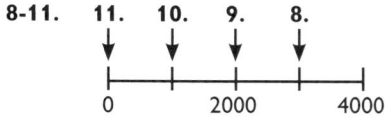

12. 100
13. 1000
14. 1000
15. 1000
16. 100
17. 100

Set C

1. 600, 1000
2. 1100, 1000
3. 8900, 9000
4. 900, 1000
5. 6900, 7000
6. 2900, 3000
7. 4400, 4000
8. 7399

9. 7450
10. 6905
11. 7070
12. 8549
13. 8450
14. If there are fewer than 8500 fans (8450-8499), this rounds down to 8000.

Pages 12-13: Solving Problems with Numbers

Set A

1. 90
2. 100
3. 68
4. 6
5. 3

6. 2038
7. −1
8. 6
9. £1105, £1255, £1599
10. £5490

Set B

1. 5830 km, 5800 km. 5830 km is bigger.
2. −5
3. Mr. Irons
4. 4

5. 6 tables
6. 1260
7. Week 1
8. 1000 + 2000 + 2000 = 5000
9. 99
10. 249

Set C

1. 5547
2. 4000
3. 210
4. 10

5. 120 m
6. £50
7. −14 °C

8. −36 °C
9. 8900
10. 6500

Page 14: Number and Place Value — Review 2

1. 1926, 2985, 3004
2. 7829, 8632, 8985
3. 2351, 2978, 3186, 3521
4. 5781, 6700, 6724, 6813
5. 1209, 1886, 1902, 1996
6. 4512, 4527, 4572, 4752

7. <
8. >
9. >
10. <
11. 90
12. 620
13. 1080
14. 560
15. 8730
16. 9000
17. 720
18. 8460
19. 2620
20. 1810
21. 300
22. 1400
23. 6600
24. 2900
25. 4500
26. 4000
27. 1000
28. 3000

29. 4000
30. 3000
31. 4000
32. 8000
33. 9000
34. 9000
35. 50, 149
36. 3850, 3949
37. 9050, 9149
38. 4450, 4549
39. 3082 kilobytes
40. 3600 kilobytes
41. 6 °C
42. 10 °C
43. 17 °C
44. −9 °C
45. −7 °C
46. 3
47. £4983
48. £8983
49. 8660
50. 6800

Page 15: Fractions

Set A

1. $\frac{1}{3}$
2. $\frac{1}{5}$
3. $\frac{4}{5}$
4. $\frac{1}{10}$
5. $\frac{6}{10}$
6. $\frac{5}{6}$
7. $\frac{3}{4}$

8. E.g.

9. E.g.

10. E.g.

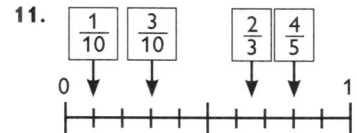

11.

Set B

1. $\frac{2}{4}$
2. $\frac{5}{7}$
3. $\frac{10}{15}$
4. $\frac{8}{12}$
5. $\frac{1}{100}$
6. $\frac{11}{12}$
7. $\frac{14}{100}$

8. $\frac{1}{4}$
9. $\frac{1}{10}$
10. $\frac{1}{2}$ or $\frac{4}{8}$
11. $\frac{1}{3}$ or $\frac{2}{6}$

12-14.

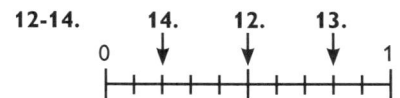

Set C

1. E.g.
2. E.g.
3. E.g.

4. 2
5. 9
6. 12
7. 10
8-10.

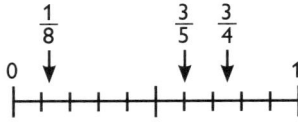

Page 16: Decimals

Set A

1. 0.5
2. 13.6
3. 40.8
4. 13.64
5. 0.12
6. 20.35
7. 63.29
8. 7
9. 5

10-11.

12. tenths
13. hundredths
14. tenths
15. tenths
16. tenths
17. hundredths

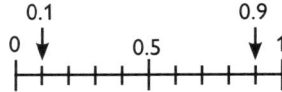

Set B

1. 4
2. 2
3-4.

5. 0.3
6. 8.1
7. 9.64
8. 2.11
9. 3.09
10. 5 tens, 0 ones and 4 tenths
11. 2 tens, 6 ones, 9 tenths and 7 hundredths
12.

Set C

1. 4
2. 6
3. 0
4. 1 tenth or 0.1
5. 9 hundredths or 0.09
6.

7-9.

10. 9.37
11. 97.3
12. 3.79

Pages 17-18: Roman Numerals

Set A

1. 1
2. 50
3. 10
4. 5
5. 2
6. 100
7. 6
8. 20
9. 60
10. I
11. I
12. X
13. V
14. LV
15. X
16. L
17. XI

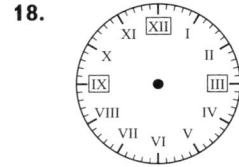

18.

19.

Set B

1. 3
2. 52
3. 71
4. XI
5. XXII
6. LXVI
7. XXXIII
8. LV
9. XVII
10. LXI
11. XXVI

12.

II	IV	VI
2	4	6

13.

V	X	XV
5	10	15

14.

C	LXXV	L
100	75	50

15.

XC	LXXX	LXX
90	80	70

16.

LI	L	XLIX
51	50	49

17. XLV
18. LXV
19. XLII
20. LXII

Set C

1. XL
2. XLVI
3. XCIV
4. XII
5. XCVI
6. X
7. XIX
8. XII
9. LVII
10. LXXXII
11. LVI

12. XLII
13. XCV
14. XVI
15. LI, LV
16. LVIII
17. LIV, LVI, LIX
18. XLVI
19. XCIII
20. XLV
21. XC

Page 19: Number and Place Value — Review 3

1. $\frac{1}{4}$
2. $\frac{2}{5}$
3. $\frac{3}{5}$
4. $\frac{3}{7}$
5. $\frac{7}{10}$
6. $\frac{9}{10}$
7. B
8. D
9. A
10. C
11. E.g.
12. E.g.
13. E.g.
14. E.g.
15. $\frac{1}{4}$
16. $\frac{5}{6}$
17. $\frac{1}{2}$ or $\frac{3}{6}$
18. $\frac{2}{3}$
19. $\frac{3}{4}$ or $\frac{9}{12}$

20. $\frac{1}{3}$ or $\frac{2}{6}$
21. 5.24
22. 15.7
23. 79.81
24. 0.9
25. 25.02
26. 8 tenths or 0.8
27. 1 tenth or 0.1
28. 7 hundredths or 0.07
29. 3 tenths or 0.3
30. 2 hundredths or 0.02
31. 5 hundredths or 0.05
32. C
33. B
34. A
35. D
36. *see below*
37. 100
38. 2
39. 4
40. 12
41. 14
42. 65
43. 76
44. 91
45. III
46. IX
47. XX
48. XXXII
49. LXIII
50. LXXXVII
51. XLIX
52. XCVIII
53. XV
54. LII
55. LXVI
56. LXXVI

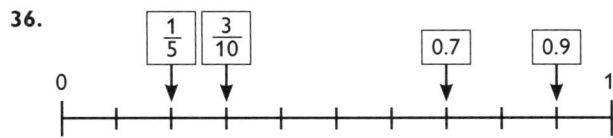

36.

Pages 20-22: Number and Place Value — Challenges

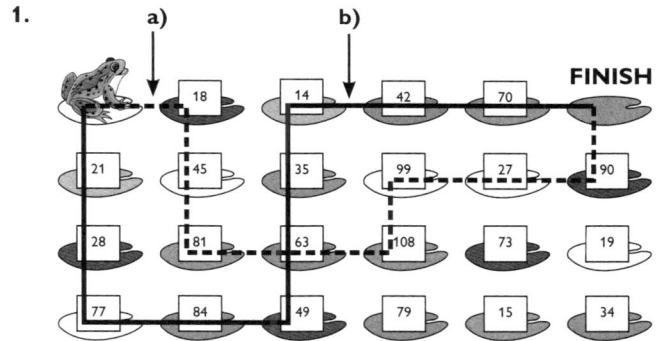

1.

   c) 63 — 63 is both a multiple of 7 and 9 (7 × 9 = 63)

2. a) 3750
   b) 704
   c) 320
   d) 9900
   e) 2025

3. −6 m

4. a)

Runner	Time (in seconds)
Eli	7993
Bill	7890
Claire	7886
Rahul	7893

   b) Claire
   c) Rahul

5. a) Glasgow
   b) Liverpool
   c) Newcastle

6. a)

Decimal	
1.45	○ ■ ■ ■ ■ △ △ △ △ △
3.25	○ ○ ○ ■ ■ △ △ △ △ △
0.71	■ ■ ■ ■ ■ ■ ■ △
1.04	○ △ △ △ △

7. a) 3
   b) 3
   c) 10
   d) 13

8. 11.7, 1.23, 15.1, 22, 3.12, 30.54

9. 9472

Section 2 — Addition and Subtraction

Page 23: Mental Addition — 1

Set A

1. 170	8. 1500	15. 60
2. 290	9. 5800	16. 70
3. 370	10. 9900	17. 30
4. 190	11. 4770	18. 500
5. 490	12. 6910	19. 300
6. 670	13. 8820	20. 300
7. 880	14. 8070	21. 200

Set B

1. 987	8. 5448	15. 800
2. 220	9. 2150	16. 700
3. 420	10. 3130	17. 60
4. 720	11. 4320	18. 60
5. 810	12. 6690	19. 90
6. 944	13. 7332	20. 900
7. 1215	14. 9645	21. 800

Set C

1. 8884	8. 1000	15. 70
2. 7205	9. 990	16. 80
3. 8422	10. 3360	17. 90
4. 8108	11. 5090	18. 700
5. 9114	12. 7192	19. 500
6. 7337	13. 8421	20. 900
7. 9049	14. 9216	21. 800

Page 24: Mental Addition — 2

Set A

1. 177	8. 1890	15. 3
2. 288	9. 3970	16. 7
3. 499	10. 4720	17. 9
4. 596	11. 5925	18. 30
5. 1789	12. 8799	19. 5
6. 2986	13. 9828	20. 3
7. 3095	14. 9834	21. 70

Set B

1. 223	8. 2130	15. 50
2. 315	9. 5169	16. 70
3. 622	10. 6498	17. 40
4. 806	11. 7237	18. 800
5. 2798	12. 9249	19. 800
6. 4925	13. 9393	20. 400
7. 5219	14. 9953	21. 800

Set C

1. 4059	8. 4953	15. 81
2. 5489	9. 4540	16. 87
3. 1389	10. 7281	17. 69
4. 8091	11. 9236	18. 910
5. 2920	12. 3214	19. 507
6. 9495	13. 6219	20. 380
7. 2145	14. 9271	21. 590

Page 25: Mental Subtraction — 1

Set A

1. 140	8. 2200	15. 60
2. 340	9. 5200	16. 40
3. 610	10. 4150	17. 50
4. 1530	11. 7070	18. 40
5. 2510	12. 6110	19. 700
6. 3620	13. 8220	20. 600
7. 5730	14. 9270	21. 500

Set B

1. 60	8. 2520	15. 60
2. 180	9. 1830	16. 70
3. 470	10. 4890	17. 90
4. 1680	11. 5535	18. 60
5. 2780	12. 7743	19. 700
6. 3880	13. 5727	20. 800
7. 1353	14. 8343	21. 600

Set C

1. 3764	8. 60	15. 80
2. 5004	9. 1980	16. 70
3. 8032	10. 2700	17. 70
4. 3926	11. 4880	18. 800
5. 6963	12. 5659	19. 500
6. 5892	13. 7686	20. 700
7. 7821	14. 8890	21. 600

Page 26: Mental Subtraction — 2

Set A

1. 172	8. 1220	15. 1
2. 151	9. 3320	16. 2
3. 232	10. 4410	17. 5
4. 1322	11. 5206	18. 20
5. 3513	12. 8201	19. 10
6. 5932	13. 9103	20. 60
7. 7311	14. 3900	21. 10

Set B

1. 138	8. 4860	15. 40
2. 339	9. 5302	16. 60
3. 581	10. 2280	17. 90
4. 653	11. 4097	18. 500
5. 1229	12. 7941	19. 800
6. 4772	13. 7808	20. 600
7. 5735	14. 8924	21. 800

Set C

1. 1989	8. 1839	15. 43
2. 4688	9. 2759	16. 51
3. 5275	10. 4726	17. 720
4. 8811	11. 5740	18. 620
5. 2791	12. 7935	19. 840
6. 5675	13. 7619	20. 707
7. 7783	14. 8780	21. 708

Page 27: Mental Subtraction — 3

Set A

1. 130	7. 125	12. 710
2. 530	8. 56	13. 520
3. 25	9. 350	14. 590
4. 34	10. 605	15. 3005
5. 150	11. 380	16. 450
6. 81		

Set B

1. 187	7. 189	12. 5900
2. 1910	8. 163	13. 5214
3. 84	9. 268	14. 1120
4. 432	10. 450	15. 4770
5. 618	11. 818	16. 7890
6. 395		

Set C

1. 389	7. 237	12. 3790
2. 168	8. 374	13. 560
3. 345	9. 838	14. 4143
4. 491	10. 1719	15. 4820
5. 289	11. 1078	16. 2149
6. 486		

Page 28: Addition and Subtraction — Review 1

1. 260	33. 5995	65. 70
2. 793	34. 8287	66. 800
3. 2990	35. 2944	67. 143
4. 3379	36. 4122	68. 924
5. 5360	37. 6226	69. 4322
6. 7667	38. 9417	70. 5831
7. 530	39. 55	71. 3320
8. 944	40. 37	72. 9143
9. 2940	41. 540	73. 608
10. 4734	42. 76	74. 751
11. 5388	43. 48	75. 1526
12. 9207	44. 780	76. 4683
13. 3197	45. 350	77. 6090
14. 9897	46. 811	78. 7820
15. 8040	47. 4510	79. 1455
16. 5225	48. 6719	80. 2477
17. 50	49. 5360	81. 6093
18. 30	50. 7167	82. 8886
19. 400	51. 580	83. 80
20. 80	52. 894	84. 93
21. 50	53. 1680	85. 195
22. 800	54. 3574	86. 180
23. 174	55. 3650	87. 570
24. 678	56. 7607	88. 1070
25. 3492	57. 5800	89. 885
26. 5874	58. 7850	90. 1967
27. 7980	59. 4640	91. 6330
28. 9797	60. 1826	92. 1280
29. 624	61. 40	93. 5780
30. 827	62. 50	94. 2916
31. 1794	63. 300	
32. 3639	64. 80	

Page 29: Written Addition — 1

Set A

1. 4499	6. 8178	10. 6219
2. 5876	7. 3589	11. 8291
3. 8998	8. 7672	12. 7859
4. 9797	9. 7509	13. 7199
5. 5787		

Set B

1. 6994	5. 8093	8. 9758
2. 7919	6. 8221	9. 5318
3. 6768	7. 8666	10. 8060
4. 8284		

Set C

1. 8398	6. 7250	11. 9041
2. 9081	7. 5000	12. 4421 km
3. 9832	8. 9250	13. 7436 km
4. 8123	9. 9340	14. 9310 km
5. 9720	10. 4430	

Page 30: Written Addition — 2

Set A

1. 7.8	6. 85.81	10. 582.7
2. 9.1	7. 9.5	11. 899.0
3. 97.9	8. 71.7	12. 88.19
4. 83.2	9. 89.2	13. 90.09
5. 877.6		

Set B

1. 40.2	5. 190.2	8. 338.3
2. 92.1	6. 59.42	9. 83.29
3. 748.2	7. 96.0	10. 26.64 km
4. 784.2		

Set C

1. 892.2	7. 202.9	13. 76.22
2. 890.3	8. 203.2	14. 76.63
3. 926.3	9. 900.7	15. 312.7 g
4. 87.24	10. 723.3	16. 206.4 g
5. 91.33	11. 830.3	17. 386.2 g
6. 87.21	12. 45.45	

Page 31: Written Subtraction — 1

Set A

1.	2251	6.	5391	10.	2218
2.	2321	7.	2232	11.	2271
3.	1111	8.	4081	12.	543
4.	2143	9.	3912	13.	5724
5.	3118				

Set B

1.	1226	5.	827	8.	3217
2.	1273	6.	7609	9.	7092
3.	2612	7.	4632	10.	2804
4.	4535				

Set C

1.	1947	6.	6859	10.	1638
2.	1778	7.	8888	11.	3559
3.	1894	8.	4168	12.	1668 g
4.	4789	9.	1749	13.	1849 g
5.	3679				

Page 32: Written Subtraction — 2

Set A

1.	4.2	6.	31.74	10.	254.7
2.	41.1	7.	6.2	11.	415.1
3.	4.7	8.	9.1	12.	131.5
4.	29.4	9.	24.8	13.	20.60
5.	363.5				

Set B

1.	19.0	5.	29.09	8.	44.82
2.	56.8	6.	22.46	9.	658.7
3.	131.9	7.	15.6	10.	25.82 km
4.	378.1				

Set C

1.	174.8	7.	28.59	12.	71.86
2.	437.9	8.	76.5	13.	37.18
3.	68.88	9.	574.8	14.	91.29
4.	36.76	10.	368.9	15.	£13.88
5.	38.85	11.	688.7	16.	30.68 litres
6.	118.8				

Page 33: Addition and Subtraction Review — 2

1.	7979	24.	6293	47.	1532
2.	8898	25.	7402	48.	5898
3.	7949	26.	9.2	49.	1838
4.	9598	27.	679.8	50.	2598
5.	7898	28.	70.41	51.	1693
6.	8877	29.	45.8	52.	2465
7.	7882	30.	893.5	53.	4213
8.	9001	31.	90.38	54.	7224
9.	8091	32.	94.16	55.	6166
10.	9090	33.	596.9	56.	7330
11.	7731	34.	70.25	57.	2887
12.	9126	35.	533.1 g	58.	£2454
13.	8932	36.	2613	59.	1527 ml
14.	8014	37.	1137	60.	4.6
15.	8324	38.	4243	61.	457.1
16.	9522	39.	868	62.	20.73
17.	5777	40.	3341	63.	3.1
18.	5488	41.	3242	64.	10.9
19.	5992	42.	1519	65.	427.2
20.	3275	43.	5162	66.	3.77
21.	3954	44.	843	67.	42.78
22.	7201	45.	1856	68.	15.38
23.	8025	46.	1837	69.	17.88 km

Page 34: Checking Calculations — 1

Set A

1.	11	7.	279
2.	27	8.	581
3.	103	9.	97 − 19 = 78 or 97 − 78 = 19
4.	227	10.	91 + 41 = 132
5.	27	11.	639 − 273 = 366 or 639 − 366 = 273
6.	49	12.	419 + 330 = 749

Set B

1. 154
2. 888
3. 417
4. 4792
5. 912 + 652 = 1564
6. 3922 − 784 = 3138 or 3922 − 3138 = 784
7. 8115 + 1681 = 9796
8. 46 + 29 = 75
9. 167 − 55 = 112 or 167 − 112 = 55
10. 243 + 131 = 374
11. 1017 − 263 = 754 or 1017 − 754 = 263
12. 1216 + 769 = 1985
13. 2227 − 1532 = 3759 or 2227 − 3759 = 1532

Set C

1. 293
2. 239
3. 4956
4. 2465
5. 92 + 162 = 254
6. 740 − 258 = 482 or 740 − 482 = 258
7. 1248 + 2498 = 3746
8. 6834 − 995 = 5839 or 6834 − 5839 = 995
9. 917 + 6666 = 7583
10. 9221 − 4362 = 4859 or 9221 − 4859 = 4362
11. Answer: 263
    Check: 263 + 271 = 534
12. Answer: 1799
    Check: 1799 − 749 = 1050 or 1799 − 1050 = 749
13. Answer: 9889
    Check: 9889 − 5106 = 4783 or 9889 − 4783 = 5106
14. Answer: 2174
    Check: 2174 + 7500 = 9674
15. Answer: 1914
    Check: 1914 + 842 = 2756
16. Answer: 7023
    Check: 7023 − 702 = 6321 or 7023 − 6321 = 702

Page 35: Checking Calculations — 2

Set A

1. 30 − 20
2. 80 + 40
3. 170 − 90
4. 270 + 80
5. 650 − 430
6. 1800 + 900

7.

- 57 + 38 → 100
- 173 − 19 → 150
- 251 + 248 → 500
- 879 − 176 → 700
- 558 + 333 → 890
- 427 − 174 → 260

8. Mike got the answers to B and C wrong.

Set B

1. 160 + 80
2. 220 − 20
3. 530 + 170
4. 630 − 370
5. 1400 + 940
6. 2700 − 450
7. 240 + 120 = 360
8. 360 − 220 = 140
9. 1200 + 760 = 1960
10. 900 − 860 = 40
11. 1800 + 140 = 1940
12. 2700 − 640 = 2060
13. Estimate: 100 + 120 = 220
    Answer: 218
14. Estimate: 280 − 190 = 90
    Answer: 92
15. Estimate: 460 + 350 = 810
    Answer: 811
16. Estimate: 750 − 560 = 190
    Answer: 182
17. Estimate: 1600 + 330 = 1930
    Answer: 1919
18. Estimate: 4700 − 560 = 4140
    Answer: 4181

Set C

1. 570 − 270 = 300
2. 3900 + 300 = 4200
3. 240 + 680 = 920
4. 1300 + 700 = 2000
5. 5800 − 2900 = 2900
6. 2800 − 190 = 2610
7. Estimate: 120 + 220 = 340
   Answer: 332
8. Estimate: 370 − 150 = 220
   Answer: 221
9. Estimate: 860 − 360 = 500
   Answer: 494
10. Estimate: 610 + 400 = 1010
    Answer: 1010
11. Estimate: 5300 + 4600 = 9900
    Answer: 9901
12. Estimate: 9800 − 7400 = 2400
    Answer: 2394
13. 1900 + 430 = 2330
14. Higher — both numbers in the calculation were rounded up and then added, so the estimate must be higher than the actual answer.
15. The actual answer must be lower than 2330. Ravi's answer is higher than this, so it must be wrong.

Pages 36-37: Addition and Subtraction Problems — 1

Set A

1. 415
2. 875
3. 127
4. 781
5. 136
6. 568
7. 8938
8. 325 m
9. 825 m
10. 125 m
11. £4346
12. £3895
13. £2034
14. 235

Set B

1. 9958
2. 2932
3. 2608
4. 5511
5. 7518
6. £3489
7. 9355
8. £1130
9. £1137
10. £652
11. £2078

Set C

1. 1394 km
2. 650 km
3. 589 km
4. 2679
5. 8153
6. 9206
7. 4603
8. 989 hours
9. 1569
10. 2721

Pages 38-39: Addition and Subtraction Problems — 2

Set A

1. 10.2 g
2. 14.2 kg
3. 98.8 kg
4. 55.8 kg
5. 3.5 litres
6. 29.9 litres
7. 1.12 km
8. 14.69 km
9. 8.54 km
10. 1.32 m
11. 15.58 m
12. 10.31 m
13. 15.49

Set B

1. 169.3 m
2. 68.3 m
3. 81.7 litres
4. 453.8 litres
5. 27.91 m
6. 36.4 miles
7. 18.8 miles
8. 38.9 miles
9. 81.4 kg

Set C

1. 4.85 kg
2. 809.1 m
3. 999.3 miles
4. 46.9 miles
5. 9.9 cm
6. 38.8 cm
7. 425.6 m
8. 45.69

Page 40: Addition and Subtraction — Review 3

1. 53
2. 142
3. 235
4. 478
5. 746
6. 1573
7. 3726
8. 7509
9. 369 − 242 = 127 or 369 − 127 = 242
10. 228 + 255 = 483
11. 1423 − 486 = 937 or 1423 − 937 = 486
12. 1068 + 1746 = 2814
13. Answer: 209
    Check: 209 + 284 = 493
14. Answer: 2632
    Check: 2632 − 847 = 1785 or 2632 − 1785 = 847
15. Answer: 6131
    Check: 6131 + 816 = 6947
16. Answer: 1993
    Check: 1993 − 1012 = 981 or 1993 − 981 = 1012
17. Answer: 401
    Check: 401 + 1328 = 1729
18. Answer: 2922
    Check: 2922 − 172 = 2750 or 2922 − 2750 = 172
19. 372 + 529 → 900
    1293 − 796 → 500
    736 + 802 → 1540
    2729 − 1617 → 1100
20. 190 − 80
21. 480 + 320
22. 2300 − 1500
23. 3000 + 4000
24. 1900 − 970
25. 4900 + 580
26. Estimate: 270 + 130 = 400
    Answer: 402
27. Estimate: 590 − 270 = 320
    Answer: 312
28. Estimate: 2200 + 750 = 2950
    Answer: 3001
29. Estimate: 7600 − 3100 = 4500
    Answer: 4491
30. 229
31. 544
32. 2424
33. 3133
34. 3633
35. 7308
36. 4.35 kg
37. 13.16 kg
38. 428.6
39. 178.1 ml

Pages 41-43: Addition and Subtraction — Challenges

1. a) 841
   b) 2185
   c) 9375
   d) E.g.
      841 − 200 − 50 − 9 = 582
      2185 + 7 + 30 + 400 + 3000 = 5622
      9375 − 7000 − 500 − 90 − 2 = 1883

2.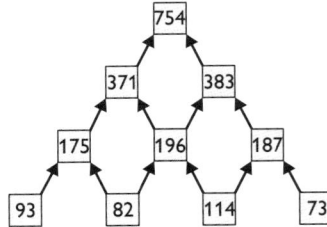

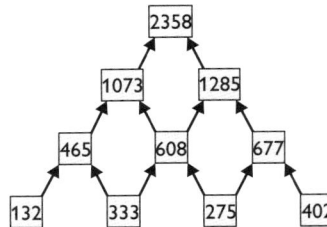

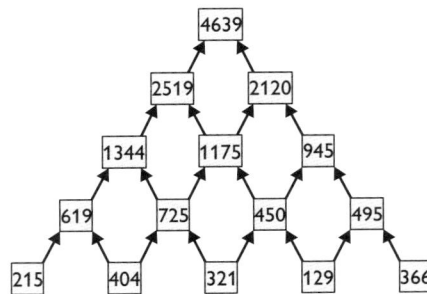

3.

600	1200	1500	100
900	700	400	1400
300	1300	1000	800
1600	200	500	1100

4. a) E.g. 1357 + 2468 = 3825
   b) E.g. 1572 + 3684 = 5256
   c) E.g. 1573 + 2684 = 4257
5. a) 1200
   b) 550
   c) 2300
   d) 4700
6. a) Emma, Maxine and Karim
   b) Catriona, Gerard and Lisa

7.

1	2	3	4	5	6	7	8	9	0
⬠	⊞	⧉	✕	⊞	◇	◈	⋈	⊡	⊗

   a) 1195
   b) 6119
   c) 7934
   d) 1159

Section 3 — Multiplication and Division

Page 44: The 6 Times Table

Set A

1.	18	7.	2 × 6 = 12	13.	24
2.	24	8.	6 × 6 = 36	14.	54
3.	48	9.	6	15.	66
4.	42	10.	42	16.	true
5.	54	11.	60	17.	false
6.	72	12.	5		

Set B

1.	12	8.	1	15.	24
2.	36	9.	9	16.	36
3.	42	10.	8	17.	54
4.	72	11.	11	18.	18
5.	18	12.	18	19.	54
6.	30	13.	30		
7.	60	14.	42		

Set C

1.	3	7.	54	13.	42
2.	42	8.	5	14.	72
3.	4	9.	11	15.	24
4.	60	10.	2	16.	36
5.	7	11.	8	17.	60
6.	72	12.	6	18.	66

Page 45: The 7 Times Table

Set A

1.	21	7.	2 × 7 = 14	13.	56
2.	35	8.	5 × 7 = 35	14.	42
3.	56	9.	1	15.	84
4.	70	10.	28	16.	true
5.	77	11.	63	17.	false
6.	84	12.	3		

Set B

1.	7	8.	4	15.	35
2.	21	9.	6	16.	42
3.	14	10.	7	17.	84
4.	56	11.	63	18.	10
5.	35	12.	84	19.	8
6.	77	13.	14		
7.	70	14.	42		

Set C

1.	10	8.	2	14.	28
2.	35	9.	11	15.	35
3.	77	10.	6	16.	56
4.	7	11.	3	17.	84
5.	56	12.	12		
6.	3	13.	8		
7.	9				

Page 46: The 9 Times Table

Set A

1.	27	7.	2 × 9 = 18	13.	54
2.	45	8.	5 × 9 = 45	14.	63
3.	54	9.	36	15.	108
4.	81	10.	99	16.	27, 45, 63
5.	90	11.	3		
6.	108	12.	81		

Set B

1.	45	7.	36	13.	108
2.	72	8.	3	14.	99
3.	18	9.	4	15.	true
4.	27	10.	7	16.	true
5.	90	11.	11	17.	72
6.	81	12.	72	18.	6

Set C

1.	18	7.	12	13.	Yes
2.	4	8.	63	14.	No
3.	6	9.	81	15.	Yes
4.	1	10.	99	16.	True
5.	45	11.	5	17.	False
6.	5	12.	12		

Page 47: The 11 Times Table

Set A

1.	44	7.	1	12.	33
2.	55	8.	2 × 11 = 22	13.	88
3.	77	9.	4 × 11 = 44	14.	132
4.	99	10.	6 × 11 = 66	15.	true
5.	110	11.	11	16.	false
6.	132				

Set B

1.	55	7.	44	13.	22
2.	77	8.	6	14.	121
3.	66	9.	1	15.	false
4.	99	10.	3	16.	true
5.	44	11.	10	17.	121
6.	132	12.	77	18.	12

Set C

1.	77	8.	3	15.	66
2.	5	9.	66	16.	88
3.	121	10.	9	17.	55
4.	1	11.	110	18.	121
5.	2	12.	12	19.	132
6.	88	13.	8		
7.	2	14.	132		

Page 48: The 12 Times Table

Set A

1. 24
2. 48
3. 72
4. 96
5. 132
6. 144

7. 1
8. 2 × 12 = 24
9. 5 × 12 = 60
10. 3 × 12 = 36
11. 84

12. 120
13. 72
14. 108
15. false
16. true

Set B

1. 84
2. 48
3. 24
4. 60
5. 36
6. 96

7. 132
8. 1
9. 6
10. 5
11. 4
12. 12

13. 10
14. 8
15. 9
16. 7
17. 60
18. 2

Set C

1. 48
2. 3
3. 6
4. 2
5. 72
6. 9

7. 144
8. 2
9. 5
10. 10
11. 7

12. 11
13. 8
14. 96
15. 84
16. 60

Page 49: Times Tables

Set A

1. 3 × 6 = 18
2. 5 × 11 = 55
3. 6 × 9 = 54
4. 0
5. 12, 18, 36, 54, 66
6. 18, 36, 45, 54

7. 18, 36, 54
8.
9.
10.

is the same as:

Set B

1. 56
2. 54
3. 110
4. 48
5. 0
6. 36

7. 144
8. 8 × 6, 6 × 8, 4 × 12, 12 × 4
9. <
10. <

11. 27
12. 20
13. 72
14. 31
15. 36

Set C

1. 88
2. 6
3. 7
4. 6
5. 12
6. 8
7. 7
8. Bobbi: 36 Cat: 72

9.

is the same as:

10. 10
11. 24
12. 30
13. 11
14. 36

Page 50: Multiplication and Division — Review 1

1. 4 × 6 = 24
2. 5 × 6 = 30
3. 18
4. 6
5. 7
6. 66
7. 2
8. 5
9. 12
10. 48
11. 3
12. 9
13. 14
14. 28
15. 7
16. 49
17. 63
18. 84
19. 56
20. 42
21. 77
22. 110
23. 3
24. 5
25. 9
26. 27
27. 9
28. 4
29. 72
30. 2
31. 12
32. 0
33. 63
34. 90
35. 11
36. 7
37. 22, 33, 55, 77 — they are repeated numbers (allow reasons such as 2 × 11 = 22)
38. 45, 63, 81 — the digits add up to 9 (allow reasons such as 5 × 9 = 45)
39. true
40. false
41. true
42. false
43. true
44. true
45. 24
46. 60
47. 84
48. 108
49. 132
50. 144
51. 10
52. 3
53. 6
54. 4
55. 56
56. 5
57. =
58. <
59. >
60. =
61. <
62. =
63. 20
64. 70
65. 132
66. 12
67. 63
68. 84

Page 51: Factor Pairs

Set A

1. 6
2. 3
3. 1 and 6, 2 and 3
4. 11
5. 1
6. 1 and 22, 2 and 11

7. 1 and 12, 2 and 6, 3 and 4
8. 1, 3
9. 1, 2, 4
10. 1 × 5 = 5

11. 1 × 7 = 7
12. 1 × 11 = 11
13. 1 × 18 = 18
   2 × 9 = 18
   3 × 6 = 18

Set B

1. 1 and 10, 2 and 5
2. 1 and 15, 3 and 5
3. 1, 5

4. 1 × 17 = 17
5. 1 × 19 = 19
6. 1 × 20 = 20
7. 2 × 10 = 20
8. 4 × 5 = 20

9. 1, 3, 7, 21
10. 1, 5, 25
11. 2 × 12 = 24
   3 × 8 = 24
   4 × 6 = 24

Set C

1. 1 × 36 = 36
   2 × 18 = 36
   3 × 12 = 36
   4 × 9 = 36
   6 × 6 = 36
2. 31
3. 32
4. 1, 2, 4, 5, 8, 10, 20, 40

5. 1, 2, 3, 6, 7, 14, 21, 42
6. 1, 3, 5, 9, 15, 45
7. 24 teams of 2, 16 teams of 3, 12 teams of 4, 8 teams of 6

8. 29 teams of 2
9. 28 teams of 2, 14 teams of 4, 8 teams of 7
10. 30 teams of 2, 20 teams of 3, 15 teams of 4, 12 teams of 5, 10 teams of 6

Page 52: Mental Multiplication — 1

Set A

1. 60
2. 200, 200
3. 100, 100
4. 180, 180
5. 420, 420

6. 50, 70
7. 180
8. 36
9. 56

10. 48
11. 44
12. 120
13. 420

Set B

1. 49, 490
2. 60, 600
3. 48, 480
4. 21, 42
5. 120
6. 540

7. 150
8. 240
9. 64
10. 54
11. 88

12. 72
13. 720
14. 7200
15. 4
16. 10

Set C

1. 480
2. 810
3. 330
4. 450
5. 112
6. 770
7. 2400
8. 280
9. 180
10. 176
11. 1000
12. 490

13. For example, multiply the answer for 9 × 8 by 2 to get 9 × 16. Then multiply that answer by 10 to get 90 × 16.
14. 1440
15. Yes — for example, to get from 9 × 8 to 90 × 16 you multiply the 9 by 10 and the 8 by 2. This is the same as multiplying the 9 by 2 (to get 18) and the 8 by 10 (to get 80), which gives 18 × 80.

Page 53: Mental Multiplication — 2

Set A

1. 1200
2. 1000, 1000
3. 1400, 1400
4. 600
5. 1200
6. 1500

7. 2100
8. 800
9. 2400
10. 2400
11. No

12. Yes
13. Yes
14. Yes
15. No
16. Yes

Set B

1. 2400
2. 3500
3. 5400
4. 4500
5. 7200
6. 9000

7. 8000
8. 9 and 200
9. 6 and 500
10. 4 and 500, 10 and 200
11. 2400

12. 4000
13. 5600
14. 3200
15. 8800
16. 9600

Set C

1. 2
2. 4000
3. 6600
4. 300
5. 6
6. 700
7. 4
8. 4500
9. 7200

10. 5400 ml
11. 1800 ml
12. Multiply 2 × 4 = 8 by 100
13. Multiply 2 × 4 = 8 by 10, and then by 100
14. Multiply 2 × 4 = 8 by 10, and then by 100
15. 7200

Page 54: Mental Multiplication — 3

Set A

1. 24, 24
2. 12, 60, 60
3. 30
4. 18, 36
5. 12, 48

6. 9, 90
7. 25, 50
8. true
9. false

10. true
11. 28
12. 30
13. 48

Set B

1. 8, 56
2. 10, 30
3. 5
4. 12
5. 27
6. 80

7. 108
8. 110
9. 96
10. 0
11. 70

12. 80
13. 60
14. 80
15. 140
16. 240

Set C

1. 42
2. 110
3. 72
4. 900
5. 165

6. 2000
7. 600
8. 240
9. 120
10. 3

11. 2 × 5 × 7
12. 3 × 5 × 8, 4 × 5 × 6
13. 8, 9, 10

Page 55: Mental Division — 1

Set A

1. 2, 2
2. 3, 3
3. 8, 8
4. 5, 5
5. 12

6. 8
7. 4
8. 6
9. 5
10. 4

11. 3
12. true
13. false
14. true

Set B

1. 2, 2
2. 8, 8
3. 11, 11
4. 12
5. 9

6. 3
7. 5
8. 6
9. 5
10. 4

11. 9
12. 12
13. 10
14. 12
15. 4

Set C

1. 4
2. 7
3. 8
4. 7

5. 9
6. 3
7. 6
8. 9

9. 7
10. 11
11. 8

Page 56: Mental Division — 2

Set A

1.	20	8.	2	15.	false
2.	100	9.	160	16.	true
3.	100	10.	3	17.	false
4.	30	11.	120	18.	50
5.	10	12.	4	19.	30
6.	200	13.	3		
7.	40	14.	2800		

Set B

1.	90	7.	120	11.	120
2.	60	8.	420 ÷ 70	12.	72
3.	80	9.	210 ÷ 7,	13.	60
4.	80		360 ÷ 12	14.	12
5.	20	10.	400 ÷ 80	15.	10
6.	120				

Set C

1.	=	5.	>	9.	600 ÷ 12
2.	>	6.	=	10.	50
3.	=	7.	300 ÷ 30	11.	400
4.	>	8.	550 ÷ 5		

Page 57: Multiplication and Division — Review 2

1.	4 and 5	21.	75	42.	True
2.	3 and 6	22.	240	43.	False
3.	4 and 6	23.	60p	44.	40
4.	3 and 10,	24.	300p	45.	48
	5 and 6	25.	360p	46.	72
5.	5, 10, 20, 30	26.	100p	47.	6
6.	5, 10	27.	150p	48.	4
7.	3, 5	28.	310p	49.	8
8.	120	29.	225p	50.	11
9.	320	30.	1000	51.	80
10.	44, 440	31.	1800	52.	70
11.	24, 240	32.	1600	53.	1210
12.	72, 720	33.	2800	54.	900
13.	84, 840	34.	7200	55.	700
14.	99, 990	35.	8100	56.	800
15.	66	36.	3600	57.	6
16.	132	37.	3000	58.	12
17.	1320	38.	6000	59.	6
18.	2640	39.	3600	60.	50
19.	28	40.	True	61.	10
20.	64	41.	False		

Page 58: Grid Method Multiplication

Set A

1.
×	4
10	40
5	20
	60

2.
×	6
20	120
8	48
	168

3.
×	5
30	150
3	15
	165

4.
×	3
100	300
30	90
2	6
	396

5.
×	5
100	500
40	200
5	25
	725

6.
×	4
200	800
10	40
5	20
	860

7.	204
8.	220
9.	174
10.	972
11.	1408
12.	2502

Set B

1.
×	5
10	50
6	30
	80

2.
×	7
30	210
4	28
	238

3.
×	6
50	300
4	24
	324

4.
×	6
100	600
50	300
8	48
	948

5.
×	4
200	800
10	40
5	20
	860

6.
×	5
300	1500
20	100
4	20
	1620

7.	190
8.	224
9.	588
10.	1020
11.	2422
12.	4208

Set C

1.
×	6
20	120
6	36
	156

2.
×	7
40	280
6	42
	322

3.
×	9
80	720
6	54
	774

4.
×	6
300	1800
60	360
2	12
	2172

5.
×	9
400	3600
80	720
7	63
	4383

6.
×	9
700	6300
50	450
9	81
	6831

7.	304
8.	504
9.	792
10.	1650
11.	4122
12.	5523

Page 59: Short Multiplication — 1

Set A

1.	39	5.	476	9.	215
2.	92	6.	624	10.	156
3.	95	7.	78	11.	304
4.	238	8.	245	12.	423

Set B

1.	132	5.	513	8.	602
2.	270	6.	532	9.	536
3.	153	7.	190	10.	432
4.	234				

Set C

1.	445	6.	546	10.	413
2.	336	7.	534	11.	581
3.	582	8.	336	12.	234
4.	405	9.	711	13.	632
5.	552				

Page 60: Short Multiplication — 2

Set A

1.	268	5.	655	9.	615
2.	936	6.	2532	10.	1808
3.	884	7.	405	11.	2799
4.	852	8.	2884	12.	3192

Set B

1.	969	5.	2275	9.	2816
2.	464	6.	4314	10.	2112
3.	755	7.	1415	11.	3168
4.	2406	8.	3388		

Set C

1.	924	6.	5957	11.	1125 g
2.	2114	7.	1488	12.	1736
3.	6088	8.	4565	13.	6391
4.	4865	9.	1472	14.	3204
5.	3123	10.	750 g		

Page 61: Short Division — 1

Set A

1.	23	7.	204	12.	22
2.	21	8.	109	13.	201
3.	23	9.	32	14.	206
4.	213	10.	51	15.	91
5.	102	11.	31	16.	31
6.	306				

Set B

1.	323	6.	208	10.	91
2.	201	7.	209	11.	21
3.	103	8.	71	12.	123
4.	106	9.	81	13.	41
5.	51				

Set C

1.	309	6.	109	11.	86
2.	92	7.	109	12.	89
3.	61	8.	71	13.	104
4.	107	9.	81	14.	93
5.	71	10.	99	15.	31

Page 62: Short Division — 2

Set A

1.	14	7.	151	13.	213
2.	14	8.	117	14.	121
3.	16	9.	315	15.	171
4.	132	10.	112	16.	113
5.	121	11.	112	17.	116
6.	171	12.	119		

Set B

1.	112	6.	132	11.	62
2.	263	7.	232	12.	122
3.	27	8.	91	13.	142
4.	114	9.	228	14.	71
5.	39	10.	79	15.	62

Set C

1.	51	6.	229	11.	98
2.	98	7.	76	12.	82
3.	93	8.	89	13.	142
4.	53	9.	141	14.	128
5.	136	10.	91		

Pages 63-64: Multiplication and Division Problems — 1

Set A

1. 48	6. 10	11. 32
2. 56	7. 40	12. 36
3. 2	8. 8	13. 48
4. 5	9. 5	14. 15
5. 12	10. 30	

Set B

1. 45	5. £52	9. 200
2. 450	6. 5	10. £67
3. 150	7. 99	11. £102
4. 60	8. 1800	12. 120

Set C

1. 23 kg	4. 120	7. 93
2. 120	5. 20	8. £180
3. 40	6. 59	

Pages 65-66: Multiplication and Division Problems — 2

Set A

1. £14	6. 60	10. 112
2. £84	7. 108	11. 50
3. 22	8. 8	12. 120
4. 198	9. 80	13. 72
5. 12		

Set B

1. 50 cm	5. 12	9. 126
2. 1050 cm	6. 296	10. 259
3. 105	7. 285	11. 36
4. 35	8. 675	

Set C

1. 6	5. 23	10. 2700
2. 30 toffees,	6. 138	11. 4320
25 chocolates,	7. 207	12. 80
20 mints	8. 54	13. 75
3. 225	9. 600	14. 450
4. 525		

Page 67: Multiplication and Division — Review 3

1.

×	3
30	90
4	12
	102

2.

×	9
50	450
6	54
	504

3. 130	11. 156	30. 145
4. 318	12. 304	31. 21
5. 783	13. 495	32. 118
6. 710	14. 369	33. 123
7. 2622	15. 1020	34. 158
8. 5565	16. 2499	35. 58
9. 48	17. 3912	36. 65
10. 90	18. 5076	37. 49
	19. 252	38. 99
	20. 270	39. 168
	21. 2555	40. 72
	22. 4302	41. 34 pints
	23. 19	42. £40
	24. 50	43. 8
	25. 16	44. 144
	26. 15	45. 945 g
	27. 104	46. 90
	28. 98	47. 18
	29. 96	

Pages 68-70: Multiplication and Division — Challenges

1.

496	358
× 3	× 8
1488	2864

158	068
6)948	7)476

3. 120

4. a) 110
   b) 66

5. a) Possible answers for each pupil are below.
      (Multiplications can be in any order.)
      Dario: 1 × 6 = 2 × 3, or 1 × 8 = 2 × 4, or
              2 × 6 = 3 × 4, or 3 × 6 = 2 × 9, or
              3 × 8 = 4 × 6
      Marina: 1 × 4 = 8 ÷ 2, or 1 × 2 = 6 ÷ 3
              1 × 2 = 8 ÷ 4, or 1 × 3 = 6 ÷ 2
      Jakub: 2 × 7 = 14, or 4 × 7 = 28, or
              2 × 8 = 16, or 4 × 8 = 32, or
              2 × 9 = 18, or 4 × 9 = 36, or
              3 × 4 = 12, or 6 × 7 = 42, or
              3 × 6 = 18, or 6 × 9 = 54, or
              3 × 7 = 21, or 7 × 8 = 56, or
              3 × 8 = 24, or 7 × 9 = 63, or
              3 × 9 = 27, or 8 × 9 = 72
      Riya: 1 × 2 × 6 = 3 × 4, or 1 × 3 × 8 = 4 × 6, or
              1 × 3 × 4 = 2 × 6, or 1 × 4 × 6 = 3 × 8, or
              1 × 3 × 6 = 2 × 9, or 2 × 3 × 6 = 4 × 9, or
              1 × 2 × 9 = 3 × 6, or 3 × 4 × 6 = 8 × 9

6. a) (1, 1, 4) or (1, 2, 2) or (2, 4, 5)
   b) Lowest is 1: (1, 1, 1) or (1, 2, 5) or (4, 5, 5)

7. a)

×	1	2	3	4	5	6	7	8	9	10	11	12
1	1	2	3	4	5	6	7	8	9	10	11	12
2	2	4	6	8	10	12	14	16	18	20	22	24
3	3	6	9	12	15	18	21	24	27	30	33	36
4	4	8	12	16	20	24	28	32	36	40	44	48
5	5	10	15	20	25	30	35	40	45	50	55	60
6	6	12	18	24	30	36	42	48	54	60	66	72
7	7	14	21	28	35	42	49	56	63	70	77	84
8	8	16	24	32	40	48	56	64	72	80	88	96
9	9	18	27	36	45	54	63	72	81	90	99	108
10	10	20	30	40	50	60	70	80	90	100	110	120
11	11	22	33	44	55	66	77	88	99	110	121	132
12	12	24	36	48	60	72	84	96	108	120	132	144

   b) For example: you can only multiply 7 × 7 to get 49. So it
      only appears in the 7 row and column.
   c) 36 — for example, most numbers appear an even number
      of times, because they can be made from factor pairs.
      So to have a number appearing an odd number
      of times means it has to be 2 × 2, or 3 × 3, etc.
      Trying them all up to 12 × 12 shows that
      36 is the only one that appears five times.

Section 4 — Fractions and Decimals

Pages 71-72: Equivalent Fractions

Set A

Note: other equivalent shadings are possible for Q1-4

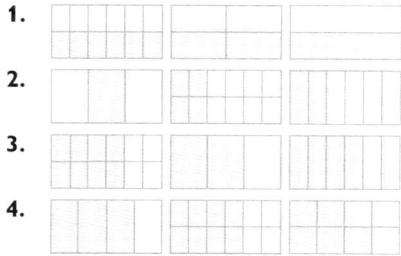

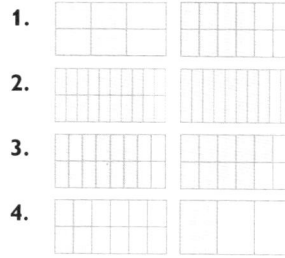

1.
2.
3.
4.
5. $\frac{4}{10} = \frac{2}{5}$
6. $\frac{5}{10} = \frac{1}{2}$
7. 3
8. 2
9. 8
10. 9
11. $\frac{2}{4} = \frac{1}{2}$
12. $\frac{6}{10} = \frac{3}{5}$
13. $\frac{1}{3} = \frac{3}{9}$
14. $\frac{1}{5} = \frac{4}{20}$

Set B

Note: other equivalent shadings are possible for Q1-5

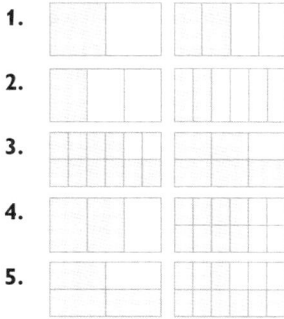

1.
2.
3.
4.
5.
6. 2
7. 4
8. $\frac{1}{2} = \frac{5}{10} = \frac{50}{100}$
9. $\frac{3}{5} = \frac{9}{15} = \frac{18}{30}$
10. $\frac{2}{3} = \frac{4}{6} = \frac{12}{18}$
11.

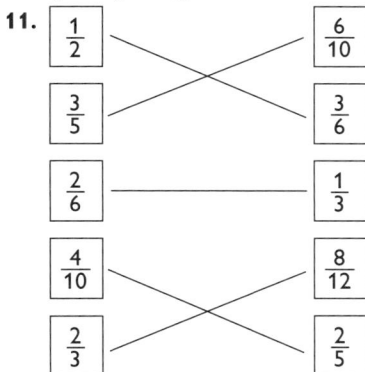

$\frac{1}{2}$	$\frac{6}{10}$
$\frac{3}{5}$	$\frac{3}{6}$
$\frac{2}{6}$	$\frac{1}{3}$
$\frac{4}{10}$	$\frac{8}{12}$
$\frac{2}{3}$	$\frac{2}{5}$

$\frac{1}{2} \to \frac{3}{6}$, $\frac{3}{5} \to \frac{6}{10}$, $\frac{2}{6} \to \frac{1}{3}$, $\frac{4}{10} \to \frac{2}{5}$, $\frac{2}{3} \to \frac{8}{12}$

Set C

Note: other equivalent shadings are possible for Q1-4

1.
2.
3.
4.
5. $\frac{1}{5} = \frac{5}{25} = \frac{20}{100}$
6. $\frac{3}{4} = \frac{9}{12} = \frac{27}{36}$
7. $\frac{3}{8} = \frac{12}{32} = \frac{15}{40}$
8. six tenths
9. ten hundredths
10. two ninths
11. four tenths
12. five sixths
13. three quarters
14. two fifths

Page 73: Counting in Fractions

Set A

1. $\frac{17}{100}$
2. $\frac{41}{100}$
3. $\frac{3}{6}$
4. $\frac{6}{10}$
5. $\frac{7}{12}$
6.
7. "**Twenty** hundredths of the shape is now shaded."
8. "**Two** tenths of the shape is now shaded."

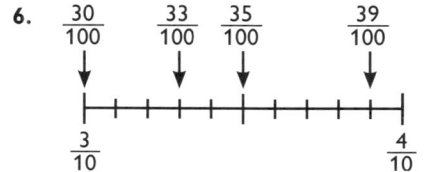

Set B

1. $\frac{46}{100}$
2. $\frac{39}{100}$
3. $\frac{3}{4}$
4. $\frac{2}{5}$
5. $\frac{1}{9}$
6. $\frac{11}{100}$
7. $\frac{7}{100}$
8.
9. $\frac{27}{100}$
10. 6
11. 14

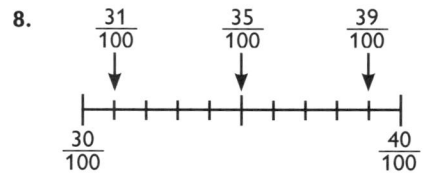

Set C

1. $\frac{67}{100}$
2. $\frac{83}{100}$
3. $\frac{4}{10}$
4. $\frac{2}{7}$
5. $\frac{3}{12}$

6-9.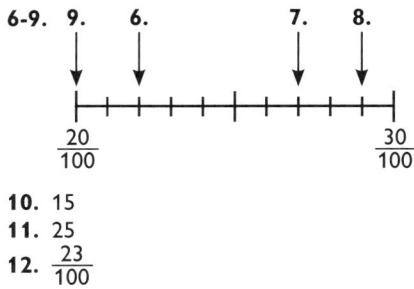

10. 15
11. 25
12. $\frac{23}{100}$

Page 74: Adding Fractions

Set A

1. $\frac{2}{3}$
2. $\frac{2}{5}$
3. $\frac{5}{6}$
4. $\frac{4}{8}$
5. $\frac{5}{10}$
6.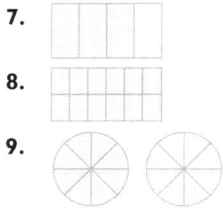

Note: other equivalent shadings are possible for Q7-9

7.
8.
9.

10. $\frac{1}{4} + \frac{2}{4} = \frac{3}{4}$
11. $\frac{5}{8} + \frac{1}{8} = \frac{6}{8}$
12. $\frac{3}{10} + \frac{7}{10} = \frac{10}{10} = 1$
13. $\frac{6}{8} + \frac{3}{8} = \frac{9}{8}$
14. $\frac{4}{9} + \frac{9}{9} = \frac{13}{9}$

Set B

1. $\frac{6}{9}$
2. $\frac{4}{5}$
3. $\frac{7}{12}$
4. $\frac{12}{15}$
5. $\frac{11}{10}$
6. nine tenths
7. seven eighths
8. four fifths

9. twelve tenths
10. eleven twelfths
11. eleven hundredths
12. $\frac{6}{7} + \frac{1}{7} + \frac{3}{7} = \frac{10}{7}$
13. $\frac{4}{9} + \frac{5}{9} + \frac{3}{9} = \frac{12}{9}$
14. $\frac{1}{5} + \frac{1}{5} + \frac{3}{5} = 1$
15. $1\frac{1}{5} + \frac{3}{5} = 1\frac{4}{5}$
16. $1\frac{5}{9} + \frac{3}{9} = 1\frac{8}{9}$

Set C

1. $\frac{13}{11}$
2. $\frac{8}{5}$
3. $\frac{14}{10}$
4. $1\frac{2}{3}$
5. $1\frac{5}{6}$
6. five quarters
7. seven quarters
8. five thirds
9. fifteen tenths

10. one and five eighths
11. two and seven tenths
12. $\frac{1}{2} + \frac{1}{2} + \frac{3}{2} = \frac{5}{2}$
13. $\frac{2}{6} + \frac{5}{6} + \frac{4}{6} = \frac{11}{6}$
14. $1\frac{4}{7} + \frac{2}{7} = 1\frac{6}{7}$
15. $1\frac{5}{12} + 1\frac{3}{12} = 2\frac{8}{12}$
16. $\frac{5}{6} + \frac{2}{6} = \frac{14}{12}$

Page 75: Subtracting Fractions

Set A

1. $\frac{3}{6}$
2. $\frac{2}{5}$
3. $\frac{1}{10}$
4. $\frac{7}{8}$
5. $\frac{11}{10}$

Note: other equivalent shadings are possible for Q6-9

6.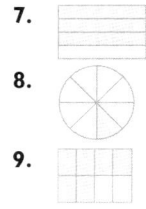

7.
8.
9.

10. $\frac{8}{10} - \frac{2}{10} = \frac{6}{10}$
11. $\frac{6}{9} - \frac{4}{9} = \frac{2}{9}$
12. $\frac{3}{5} - \frac{1}{5} = \frac{2}{5}$
13. $\frac{10}{6} - \frac{4}{6} = \frac{6}{6} = 1$
14. $\frac{7}{4} - \frac{1}{4} = \frac{6}{4}$

Set B

1. $\frac{4}{7}$
2. 0
3. $\frac{3}{9}$
4. $\frac{13}{12}$
5. $\frac{2}{3}$
6. one third
7. three tenths
8. one eighth
9. two tenths

10. four sixths
11. two sevenths
12. seven fifths
13. $\frac{6}{7} - \frac{5}{7} = \frac{1}{7}$
14. $\frac{9}{10} - \frac{4}{10} = \frac{5}{10}$
15. $\frac{8}{5} - \frac{2}{5} = \frac{6}{5}$
16. $1\frac{3}{9} - \frac{2}{9} = 1\frac{1}{9}$
17. $1\frac{5}{12} - \frac{3}{12} = 1\frac{2}{12}$

Set C

1. $\frac{6}{5}$
2. $\frac{5}{2}$
3. $1\frac{1}{8}$
4. $1\frac{2}{10}$
5. $1\frac{3}{20}$
6. six quarters
7. five thirds
8. seven sixths
9. one and two fifths

10. one and two tenths
11. two and seven fifteenths
12. $\frac{12}{10} - \frac{5}{10} - \frac{2}{10} = \frac{5}{10}$
13. $\frac{5}{2} - \frac{4}{2} - \frac{1}{2} = 0$
14. $\frac{25}{12} - \frac{15}{12} - \frac{7}{12} = \frac{3}{12}$
15. $\frac{10}{8} - \frac{3}{8} - \frac{1}{8} = \frac{6}{8}$
16. $\frac{30}{20} - \frac{15}{20} - \frac{13}{20} = \frac{2}{20}$

Pages 76-77: Fractions of Amounts

Set A

1. 5
2. 6
3. 30
4. 12
5. 4
6. 4
7. 6
8. 9
9.

(any 10 squares shaded)

10. "Roopesh plays 140 ÷ 10 = 14 notes correctly."
11. 2
12. 6
13. 12
14. 4

Set B

1. 5
2. 16
3. 12
4. 15
5. 16
6. 11
7. 21
8. 14
9. 60
10. 20
11. 22

Set C

1. $\frac{7}{8}$ of 64 = 56
2. $\frac{2}{8}$ of 64 = 16
3. five sevenths of 56 = 40
4. three sevenths of 56 = 24
5. 6
6. 15
7. 25
8. 22
9. 30
10. 18

Page 78: Fractions and Decimals — Review 1

Note: other equivalent shadings are possible for Q1-3

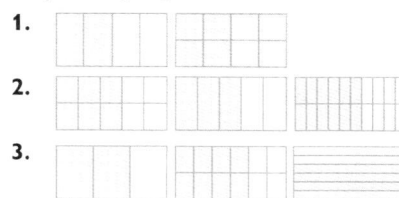

1.

2.

3.

4. $\frac{1}{6} = \frac{2}{12}$
5. $\frac{10}{15} = \frac{2}{3}$
6. $\frac{2}{3} = \frac{14}{21}$
7. $\frac{1}{10} = \frac{4}{40}$
8. $\frac{1}{8} = \frac{2}{16} = \frac{3}{24}$
9. $\frac{1}{5} = \frac{2}{10} = \frac{20}{100}$
10. $\frac{3}{4} = \frac{6}{8} = \frac{12}{16}$
11. $\frac{3}{7} = \frac{15}{35} = \frac{21}{49}$
12. $\frac{1}{4}$ = two eighths
13. $\frac{2}{6}$ = four twelfths
14. $\frac{20}{100}$ = two tenths
15. $\frac{12}{16}$ = three quarters
16. $\frac{3}{10}$
17. $\frac{5}{6}$
18. $\frac{8}{8}$ or 1
19. $\frac{12}{10}$ or $1\frac{2}{10}$
20. $\frac{23}{100}$
21. $\frac{29}{100}$
22. $\frac{32}{100}$
23. $\frac{16}{100}$
24. $\frac{26}{100}$
25. $\frac{3}{7}$
26. $\frac{11}{12}$
27. $2\frac{3}{5}$
28. six sevenths
29. $\frac{8}{3}$
30. $\frac{13}{9}$
31. $\frac{21}{10}$
32. twenty-six tenths
33. $\frac{2}{8}$
34. $\frac{2}{20}$
35. $\frac{3}{4}$
36. four eighths
37. $1\frac{1}{6}$
38. $1\frac{1}{5}$
39. $4\frac{6}{20}$
40. seventeen twelfths
41. 8
42. 6
43. 18
44. 40
45. 75
46. 36
47. 24
48. 180
49. 50

Page 79: Writing Fractions as Decimals — 1

Set A

1. 0.2
2. 0.1
3. 0.6
4. 0.9
5. 0.3
6. 8.1
7. 0.4
8. 0.1
9. 0.9
10. 0.5
11. 0.7

12.

Set B

1. 0.9
2. 1.2
3. 2.1
4. 8.7
5. 3.1
6. 4.8
7. $1\frac{1}{10} = 1.1$
8. $1\frac{8}{10} = 1.8$
9. $1\frac{4}{10} = 1.4$

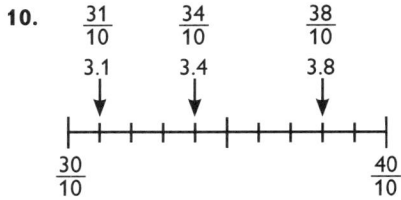

10.

$\frac{31}{10}$	$\frac{34}{10}$	$\frac{38}{10}$
3.1	3.4	3.8

$\frac{30}{10}$ $\frac{40}{10}$

Set C

1. 11.6
2. 5.8
3. 17.2
4. 5.1
5. 4.2
6. 1.6
7. 1.9
8. 3.1
9. 2.4
10. 0.1

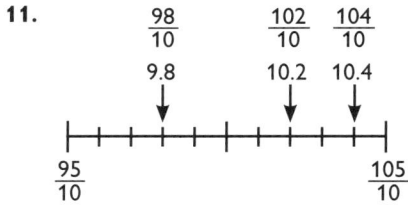

11.

$\frac{98}{10}$	$\frac{102}{10}$	$\frac{104}{10}$
9.8	10.2	10.4

$\frac{95}{10}$ $\frac{105}{10}$

Page 80: Writing Fractions as Decimals — 2

Set A

1. 0.03
2. 0.09
3. 0.08
4. 0.06
5. 0.04
6. 0.01
7. 0.12
8. 0.05
9. 0.09
10. 0.08

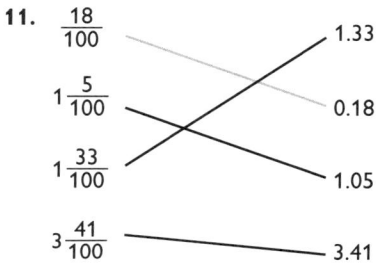

11.
$\frac{18}{100}$ 1.33
$1\frac{5}{100}$ 0.18
$1\frac{33}{100}$ 1.05
$3\frac{41}{100}$ 3.41

Set B

1. 0.16
2. 0.18
3. 0.9
4. 0.21
5. 1.29
6. 3.06
7. 49
8. 18
9. 94
10. 20

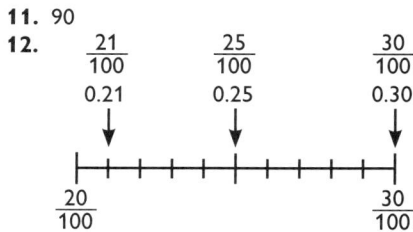

11. 90

12.

$\frac{21}{100}$	$\frac{25}{100}$	$\frac{30}{100}$
0.21	0.25	0.30

$\frac{20}{100}$ $\frac{30}{100}$

Set C

1. 55.12
2. 27.19
3. 1.26
4. 20.37
5. 31.2
6. 0.1
7. 0.98
8. 0.19

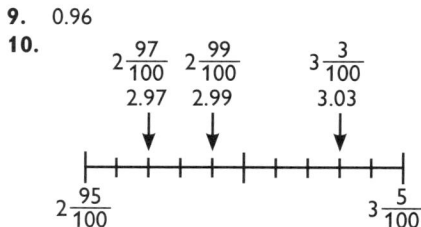

9. 0.96

10.

$2\frac{97}{100}$	$2\frac{99}{100}$	$3\frac{3}{100}$
2.97	2.99	3.03

$2\frac{95}{100}$ $3\frac{5}{100}$

Page 81: Writing Fractions as Decimals — 3

Set A

1. 0.75
2. 1.25
3. 2.75
4. 4.5
5. 6.75
6. 1.25
7. 1.75
8. 2.5

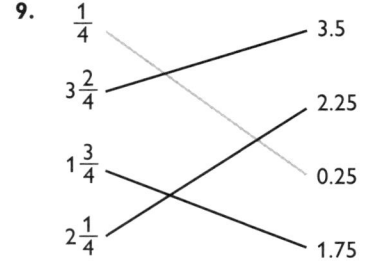

9.
$\frac{1}{4}$ 3.5
$3\frac{2}{4}$ 2.25
$1\frac{3}{4}$ 0.25
$2\frac{1}{4}$ 1.75

Set B

1. 1.5
2. 7.75
3. 14.25
4. 1.75
5. 2.5
6. 3.25
7. $1\frac{2}{4} = 1.5$

8. $2\frac{3}{4} = 2.75$
9. $2\frac{1}{4} = 2.25$
10. 3.75
11. 1.25
12. 2.75

Set C

1. 10.25
2. 15.25
3. 5.5
4. 2.75
5. 5.5
6.
7.
8.
9. 2.75

Page 82: Dividing by 10 and 100

Set A

1. 8
2. 2.6
3. 8.5
4. 0.7
5. 0.11
6. 0.38
7. 0.52
8. 0.01
9. 4
10. 1.6
11. 0.9
12. 0.8
13. 0.02
14. 0.35
15.

Start Number	÷ 10	÷ 100
90	9	0.9
17	1.7	0.17
34	3.4	0.34
28	2.8	0.28
11	1.1	0.11
3	0.3	0.03

Set B

1. 5
2. 0
3. 7
4. 9
5. 9
6. 6
7. 7.7
8. 6.1
9. 10
10. 100
11. 100
12. 100
13. 100
14. 1.4
15. 0.31
16. 0.04

Set C

1. true
2. false
3. true
4. true
5. 25
6. 61
7. 100
8. 2
9. 4 tenths and 0 hundredths
10. 5 tenths and 5 hundredths
11. 10
12. 100
13. 100
14. 0.04

Page 83: Fractions and Decimals — Review 2

1. 0.7
2. 0.2
3. 0.1
4. 8.6
5. 2.1
6. 1.2
7. 8.3
8. 1.4
9. 5.2
10. 9.1
11. $2\frac{5}{10}$ = 2.5
12. $3\frac{2}{10}$ = 3.2
13. see below
14. 0.11
15. 0.07
16. 0.13
17. 3.17
18. 5.27
19. 2.09
20. 14.2
21. 5.68
22. 32.09
23. see below
24. 0.12
25. 0.07
26. 0.18
27. 25
28. 70
29. 100
30. 88
31. 0.75
32. 6.75
33. 1.25
34. 35.5
35. 5.5
36. 2.75
37. 6.25
38. 5.5
39. $2\frac{2}{4}$ = 2.5
40. $3\frac{1}{4}$ = 3.25
41. 4
42. 3.9
43. 2.3
44. 0.8
45. 0.78
46. 0.36
47. 0.99
48. 0.04
49. 10
50. 100
51. 17
52. 100
53. 10
54. 46
55. 66
56. 100

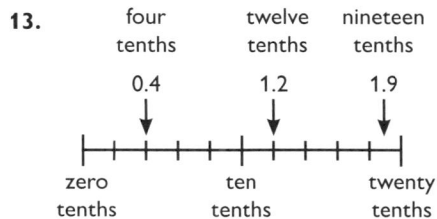

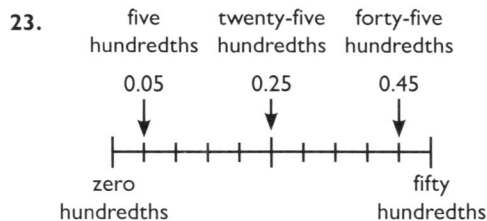

13.

	four tenths	twelve tenths	nineteen tenths
	0.4	1.2	1.9

zero tenths   ten tenths   twenty tenths

23.

	five hundredths	twenty-five hundredths	forty-five hundredths
	0.05	0.25	0.45

zero hundredths   fifty hundredths

Page 84: Counting in Decimals

Set A

1.	0.5	**6.**	0.21	**11.**	12.77
2.	0.8	**7.**	10	**12.**	0.1
3.	1.2	**8.**	9	**13.**	0.2
4.	0.14	**9.**	0.86	**14.**	0.1
5.	0.19	**10.**	2.22		

Set B

1.	1.35	**7.**	7	**12.**	2.59
2.	1.75	**8.**	10	**13.**	3.01, 3.02
3.	2.15	**9.**	15	**14.**	1.11, 1.14
4.	2.94	**10.**	7	**15.**	0.23, 0.03
5.	2.97	**11.**	2.1	**16.**	2, 1.6
6.	3.02				

Set C

1.	4.9	**6.**	1.16	**11.**	6.04
2.	4.24	**7.**	30.8	**12.**	9.85
3.	4.55	**8.**	0.94	**13.**	0.6
4.	5.09	**9.**	12.44	**14.**	11.88
5.	5.23	**10.**	1.07	**15.**	3.5

Page 85: Rounding Decimals

Set A

1.	7	**5.**	20	**9.**	2.9
2.	5	**6.**	31	**10.**	3.2
3.	1	**7.**	2	**11.**	1 m
4.	17	**8.**	8, 10, 12	**12.**	2 m

Set B

1.	9	**12.**	1.4
2.	2	**13.**	0.5
3.	0	**14.**	12.9
4.	37	**15.**	11.5
5.	112		
6.	13		
7.	91		

8-11.

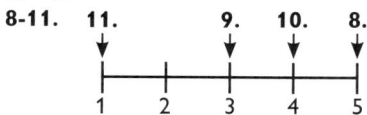

Set C

1.	50	**13.**	400
2.	523	**14.**	14
3.	701	**15.**	
4.	599		
5.	878		
6.	400		
7.	1050		
8.	10		
9.	20		
10.	40		
11.	200		
12.	94		

15.

Smallest Input	Largest Input	Output
5.5	6.4	6
98.5	99.4	99
129.5	130.4	130
0.5	1.4	1

Page 86: Ordering Decimals

Set A

1.	5.2		**8.**	0.4
2.	1.9		**9.**	5.9, 6.2, 7.1
3.	5.8		**10.**	9.8, 10.0, 10.9
4.	17.7		**11.**	0.2, 1.2, 1.8
5.	13.8		**12.**	2.1, 2.7, 12.8, 18.2
6.	0.8		**13.**	0.55, 2.25, 2.55, 5.55
7.	8.2		**14.**	0.61, 6.71, 7.62, 7.71

Set B

1.	<
2.	>
3.	<
4.	51.6, 56.2, 56.9
5.	3.12, 3.17, 3.23
6.	0.8
7.	13.2
8.	29.9
9.	7.53
10.	1.01
11.	7.91, 8.18, 8.82, 8.91
12.	3
13.	2

Set C

1.	7.6		**8.**	10.2, 18.1, 20.1, 20.3
2.	1.9		**9.**	0.33, 3.03, 3.33, 3.90
3.	12.51		**10.**	6.17, 6.27, 7.26, 7.42
4.	3.88		**11.**	0.22, 0.25, 0.52, 0.55, 2.52
5.	6.21		**12.**	1.18, 1.21, 1.28, 1.82, 2.11
6.	0.07		**13.**	6.61, 6.16, 6.11, 6.06, 6.01
7.	19.48		**14.**	6.01, 6.06, 6.11
			15.	6.16

Pages 87-88: Fraction and Decimal Problems

Set A

1.	1.5 cm	**5.**	3	**8.**	0.85 cm
2.	2 °C	**6.**	£3	**9.**	80 ml
3.	17.2 kg	**7.**	£7	**10.**	25 cm
4.	22.3 kg				

Set B

1.	Martyn	**5.**	80p	**8.**	6 m
2.	£8	**6.**	$\frac{26}{100}$	**9.**	Black
3.	£3			**10.**	White
4.	£13	**7.**	0.03 m (or 3 cm)	**11.**	0.15 mm

Set C

1.	5 minutes	**6.**	507.4 g
2.	54 minutes	**7.**	£18.00, £18.09, £17.90, £18.81, £17.54
3.	$\frac{7}{8}$	**8.**	21 months
4.	£11	**9.**	0.09 g
5.	506.5 g	**10.**	110 ml

Page 89: Fractions and Decimals — Review 3

1.	10.2	**29.**	1
2.	10.7	**30.**	99
3.	11.2	**31.**	141
4.	10.03	**32.**	200
5.	10.08	**33.**	4
6.	10.1	**34.**	50
7.	15.1	**35.**	100
8.	14.8	**36.**	39
9.	14.5	**37.**	2.6
10.	15.49	**38.**	16.4
11.	15.38	**39.**	99.4
12.	15.35	**40.**	149.7
13.	4	**41.**	<
14.	4	**42.**	>
15.	11	**43.**	<
16.	20	**44.**	<
17.	10	**45.**	>
18.	4	**46.**	<
19.	2	**47.**	1.2, 1.5, 1.9
20.	11	**48.**	2.2, 2.3, 2.8, 2.9
21.	15	**49.**	9.1, 9.9, 10.1, 10.9
22.	12	**50.**	3.06, 3.11, 3.14, 3.44, 3.61
23.	40	**51.**	5.01, 5.05, 5.15, 5.51, 5.55, 5.95
24.	21	**52.**	Craig
25.	5	**53.**	Perry
26.	12	**54.**	Papa
27.	41	**55.**	8.5 °C
28.	110	**56.**	£14

Pages 90–92: Fractions and Decimals — Challenges

1. a) $\frac{18}{100}$ or 0.18

3. a) 0.98
   b) 37
   c) 100

4. a)

Capacity of bucket	Water collected
1 litre	$\frac{3}{5}$ litres
2 litres	$\frac{6}{5}$ litres
3 litres	$\frac{9}{5}$ litres
4 litres	$\frac{12}{5}$ litres
5 litres	$\frac{15}{5}$ or 3 litres

  b) 200 days

5. a) $\frac{5}{30}$ or $\frac{1}{6}$
   b) $\frac{18}{30}$ or $\frac{3}{5}$

6. b) i) Vine 1: 17 cm (allow 16 cm or 18 cm)
        Vine 2: 10 cm (allow 9 cm or 11 cm)
        Vine 3: 16 cm (allow 15 cm or 18 cm)
        Vine 4: 13 cm (allow 12 cm or 14 cm)
    ii) Vine 1: 34 cm (allow double answer from **i)**)
        Vine 2: 50 cm (allow five times answer from **i)**)
        Vine 3: 20 cm (allow 18-22 cm)
        Vine 4: 26 cm (allow double answer from **i)**)

7. $\frac{125}{100}$ or $1\frac{25}{100}$ or $1\frac{1}{4}$ or 1.25 teaspoons

Section 5 — Measurement

Page 93: Length

Set A

1. 900 cm
2. 220 mm
3. 180 mm
4. 6000 m
5. 7500 m
6. 80 cm
7. 700 m
8. cm
9. mm
10. m
11. cm
12. mm
13. m
14. mm
15. 5 mm
16. 26 mm
17. 49 mm
18.

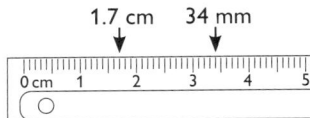

19. 34 mm

Set B

1. 185 cm
2. 142 mm
3. 800 m
4. 772 mm
5. 5200 m
6. 4 mm
7. 350 cm
8. 750
9. 2200
10. 308
11. 9950
12. 3470
13. 2790
14. 2
15. 110 mm
16. 125 mm
17. 138 mm
18. =
19. >

Set C

1. 716 mm
2. 552 cm
3. 3 cm
4. 6090 m
5. 1239 cm
6. 2880 m
7. 13.4 mm
8. cm
9. cm
10. 1240
11. m
12. mm
13. km
14. 1789
15. 2.5 m, 25 m, 0.25 km
16. 0.1 cm, 0.1 m, 100 cm
17. 70 mm, 700 mm, 75 cm
18. 1090 m, 1.19 km, 1900 m
19. 0.4 cm, 42 mm, 42 cm
20. 120 cm, 12 m, 12.7 m

Page 94: Mass

Set A

1. 2000 g
2. 3000 g
3. 6500 g
4. 9500 g
5. 1400 g
6. 8100 g
7. 5 kg
8. 1280 g
9. 1600 g
10. the blue parcel
11. 260 g

Set B

1. 8900
2. 7700
3. 2650
4. 290
5. 1070
6. 850
7. 40
8. 370 g
9. 1250 g
10. 9000 g
11. 2000 g
12. 100 g
13. 2500 g
14. 9.49 kg
15. 99 g

Set C

1. 8500 g
2. 1010 g
3. 7980 g
4. 4060 g
5. 3990 g
6. 120 g
7. 80 g
8. 4250 g and 4.25 kg
9. 5255 g
10. 35 g

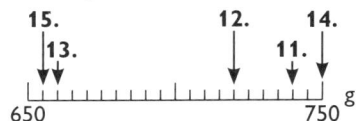

Page 95: Capacity

Set A

1. 8000 ml
2. 9000 ml
3. 1500 ml
4. 7900 ml
5. 4800 ml
6. 2600 ml
7. 5800 ml
8. 3000
9. 5000
10. 1700
11. 8200
12. 3700
13. 400
14. 900
15. Flask A, 200 ml
16. Flask B, 55 ml

Set B

1. 8400 ml
2. 9800 ml
3. 1300 ml
4. 100 ml
5. 5790 ml
6. 910 ml
7. 350 ml
8. 170 ml
9. 340 ml
10. 1400 ml
11. false
12. false
13. false
14. true

Set C

1. 2700 ml
2. 410 ml
3. 595 ml
4. 2330 ml
5. 6600 ml
6. 1770 ml
7. 664 ml
8. 8410 ml
9. Flask A, 640 ml
10. Flask A, 8900 ml
11. 850 ml, 80 ml, 800 ml
12. 650 ml
13. 90 ml
14. 770 ml

Pages 96-97: Estimating Measures

Set A

1. 2.8 kg
2. 15 cm
3. 15 cm
4. 150 mm
5. 5 mm
6. 1500 kg
7. 6 km
8. 150 litres
9. 150 g
10. Allow 80 ml-120 ml
11. Allow 240 ml-360 ml

Set B

1. 6 m
2. 350 ml
3. 4 kg
4. 10
5. 3.75 kg
6. m
7. g
8. ml
9. 6 m
10. 9 m

Set C

1. 2 litres
2. 15 m
3. 200 cm
4. 0.4 kg
5. 570 ml
6. 800 ml
7. 1600 ml
8. 10 m
9. 20 m
10. 1000 g
11. Sheriff Badge, Hand Puppet, Glowing Yo-Yo, Flying Rocket

Page 98: Measurement — Review 1

1. 300 cm
2. 850 mm
3. 2260 mm
4. 950 cm
5. 9100 m
6. 640 m
7. 1 mm
8. 30 mm
9. 54 mm
10. 68 mm
11. 20 m, 200 m, 2 km
12. 7.6 cm, 0.7 m, 760 cm
13. 9.2 cm, 920 mm, 9200 mm
14. 0.03 m, 30 cm, 3 m
15. 9000 g
16. 7800 g
17. 3200 g
18. 1120 g
19. 1820 g
20. 70 g
21. Banana
22. Book
23. Backpack
24. 7.5 kg, 7500 g
25. 3.75 kg, 3750 g
26. 0.05 kg, 50 g
27. 1.3 kg, 1300 g
28. 7000 ml
29. 800 ml
30. 150 ml
31. 9650 ml
32. 1070 ml
33. 30 ml
34. C
35. 1.8 m
36. 150 g
37. 2 litres
38. 7.5 m
39. 30 m
40. 1.5 litres
41. 1500 ml
42. 15 cm
43. 60 cm
44. 6
45. 20

Pages 99-100: Perimeter

Set A

1. 14 cm
2. 11 cm
3. 9 cm
4. 12 cm
5. 22 m
6. 140 cm
7. 2 cm
8. 6 cm
9. 4 m
10. 18 cm

Set B

1. 12 cm
2. 10 cm
3. 9 cm
4. 26 cm
5. 5 m
6. 78 m

7.

Length	Width
6 cm	1 cm
5 cm	2 cm
4 cm	3 cm

8. 48 cm
9. 24 cm
10. 60 cm

Set C

1. 11 cm, 110 mm
2. 9 cm, 90 mm
3. 11 cm, 110 mm
4. 37 m
5. 480 cm
6. 62 cm
7. E.g.

```
      8 cm
   ┌──────┬──┐
4 cm│      │  │
   └──────┴──┘
```

2 × (8 + 4) = 24 cm

8. B) 2 × (5 + 3)
9. Length = 9 m, Width = 2 m

Page 101: Area — 1

Set A

1. Shape B
2. Shape C
3. 5 squares
4. 12 squares
5. Shape A and Shape D
6. 17 cm²
7. 16 cm²
8. the same area

Set B

1. 3 cm²
2. 1 cm²
3. 4 cm²
4-5. E.g.

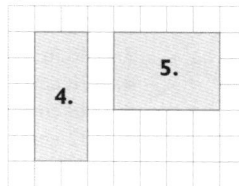

6. 8
7. 10
8. 16
9. 81

Set C

1. 6 cm²
2. 18 cm²
3. 10.5 cm²
4. 10 cm²
5. 7 times
6. 16
7. 12
8. 32

Page 102: Area — 2

Set A

1. 9
2. 12
3. 28
4. 25 cm²
5. 84 cm²
6. 80 cm²
7. 9 cm²
8. 16 cm²
9. 36 cm²

10.

Length	Width	Area
5 cm	4 cm	20 cm²
7 cm	2 cm	14 cm²
9 cm	8 cm	72 cm²

Set B

1. 80 cm²
2. 108 cm²
3. 96 cm²
4. 4 cm²
5. 5 cm²
6. 49 cm²
7. 64 cm²
8. 81 cm²
9. A and D

Set C

1. 32 cm²
2. 48 cm²
3. 240 cm²
4. 54 cm²
5. 25 cm²
6. 75 cm²
7. 150 cm²
8. 200 cm²
9. 400 cm²

Page 103: Perimeter and Area

Set A

1. C, B, A
2. C, A, B
3. 16 cm^2
4. 20 cm
5. 24 cm

6.

Width	Perimeter	Area
1 cm	4 cm	1 cm^2
3 cm	12 cm	9 cm^2
5 cm	20 cm	25 cm^2
7 cm	28 cm	49 cm^2

Set B

1.

Width	Perimeter	Area
4 cm	16 cm	16 cm^2
6 cm	24 cm	36 cm^2
8 cm	32 cm	64 cm^2
9 cm	36 cm	81 cm^2

2. 32 m
3. 48 m^2
4. 28 cm
5. 48 cm^2
6. 32 cm

Set C

1. 107 cm^2
2. 40 cm
3. 75 cm^2
4.
5.
6. 10 m
7. 32 m
8. 60 m^2

Page 104: Measurement — Review 2

1. 10 cm
2. 8 cm
3. 30 cm
4. 28 m
5. 36 cm
6. 52 cm
7. 3 m
8. 76 cm
9. 20 cm
10. 6 cm
11. 50 cm
12. 4 m
13. 0.8 m
14. 6 cm^2
15. 4 cm^2
16. 4 cm^2
17. 10 cm^2
18. 6 cm^2
19. 36 cm^2
20. 132 cm^2
21. 8
22. 24
23. 72
24. 84
25. 25 cm^2
26. 45 cm^2
27. 72 cm^2
28. 121 cm^2
29. 6 cm^2
30. 28 cm^2
31. 30 cm^2
32. 70 cm^2
33. 64 cm^2
34. 300 cm^2
35. Perim. = 24 cm, Area = 35 cm^2
36. Perim. = 20 cm, Area = 16 cm^2
37. Perim. = 44 cm, Area = 120 cm^2
38. Perim. = 22cm, Area = 30 cm^2

Page 105: Money — 1

Set A

1. £3.26
2. £5.98
3. £1.81
4. £5.65
5. £7.24
6. £3.68
7. £1.23 or 123p
8. £2.62
9. £5.26
10. £0.80
11. £18.81
12. £15.09
13. £14.93

Set B

1. £9.91
2. £40.91
3. £63.01
4. £19.32
5. £39.11
6. £8.56
7. £12.28
8. £1.78
9. £55.25
10. £23.75

Set C

1. £44.23
2. £82.21
3. £46.31
4. £1.82
5. £79.57
6. £47.89
7. £6.44
8. £10.35
9. £152.84
10. £36.86

Page 106: Money — 2

Set A

1. £2.40
2. £2.50
3. £4.00
4. £2.25
5. £3.60
6. £8.80
7. £11.10
8. £0.50
9. £0.70
10. £2.00
11. £1.10
12. £0.50
13. £2.05
14. £0.20
15. £0.84
16. £0.53
17. £9.45

Set B

1. £3.04
2. £8.50
3. £27.00
4. £3.20
5. £6.75
6. £5.04
7. £10.70
8. £2.25
9. £1.20
10. £1.60
11. £0.95
12. £0.09
13. £1.02
14. £1.04
15. £3.45
16. £8.05
17. £0.85
18. £2.55

Set C

1. £13.80
2. £16.10
3. £38.40
4. £27.30
5. £8.19
6. £17.84
7. £21.54
8. £0.60
9. £1.10
10. £0.17
11. £1.37
12. £3.07
13. £1.78
14. £0.19
15. £74.32
16. £2.76
17. £0.92

Pages 107-108: Estimating and Comparing Money

Set A

1. 3 × 20p
2. 50 × 1p
3. 2 × 50p
4. 5 × 20p
5. 5 × 10p and 10 × 1p
6. 20p + 60p + 20p = £1
7. £6
8. £1.20
9. £6
10. £9
11. £3
12. £4.50

Set B

1. 1 × 50p and 10 × 1p
2. 6 × 20p and 5 × 1p
3. £1.60
4. £2.80
5. £3.20
6. £1.60
7. £2
8. £55
9. £35
10. £10

Set C

1. three 50p coins
2. twelve 10p coins
3. eight 20p coins
4. £4.50
5. £14
6. £2
7. £21
8. £6
9. Less, because each item was rounded up.
10. £0.70

Page 109: Measurement — Review 3

1. 2.81
2. 15
3. 3.14
4. 50
5. £1.50
6. £5.03
7. £12.38
8. £20.89
9. £78.98
10. £51.71
11. £81.06
12. £80.61
13. £1.60
14. £4.35
15. £0.85
16. £20.06
17. £89.07
18. £14.82
19. £17.91
20. £11.49
21. £0.90
22. £2.70
23. £5.28
24. £30.30
25. £19.80
26. £42.90
27. £13.56
28. £38.99
29. £1.40
30. £1.19
31. £1.06
32. £0.92
33. £0.91
34. £0.47
35. 3 × 10p
36. 5 × 20p
37. 3 × 50p
38. 5 × 50p
39. £4
40. £7
41. £3 + £0.50 + £0.70 + £0.20 + £0.10 + £0.50 = £5 So £4.50 is not enough.
42. £7
43. £6
44. £24
45. £9

Page 110: Time — 1

Set A

1. 180 seconds
2. 30 seconds
3. 1200 seconds
4. 120 minutes
5. 300 minutes
6. 90 minutes
7. thirty
8. fifteen
9. six hundred
10. forty-five
11. 1 min 2 s
12. 70 s
13. 3 s

Set B

1. 45 minutes
2. 360 minutes
3. 75 minutes
4. 480 seconds
5. 1200 seconds
6. 390 seconds
7. 123 minutes
8. 58 minutes
9. true
10. true
11. false
12. true
13. false

Set C

1. 330
2. 20
3. minutes
4. 40
5. 12
6. 60
7. 90
8. 102 minutes
9. 266 minutes
10. 639 minutes
11. 325 seconds
12. 10

Page 111: Time — 2

Set A

1. 14 days
2. 35 days
3. 70 days
4. 24 months
5. 60 months
6. 15 months
7. thirty-six
8. twenty-one
9. seventy-four
10. thirty
11. 24
12. 9th May
13. 17th May

Set B

1. six
2. thirty
3. twenty-eight
4. eighty-four
5. 49 days
6. 43 days
7. 74 days
8. 144 months
9. 98 months
10. 80 months
11. 31 days
12. 26 months

Set C

1. 56
2. 108
3. 78
4. 71
5. 90
6. 120 months
7. 240 months
8. 1200 months
9. 600 months
10. 15th September
11. 5th September
12. 2nd September
13. 17th September

Pages 112-113: Clocks

Set A

1. quarter, four
2. thirteen, seven
3. 2
4. 7
5. 5
6. 9
7. 12:22
8. 1:38 pm
9. 10:54 pm
10.
11.
12.
13. 10 minutes
14. 25 minutes

Set B

1. 2:00 am
2. 11:10 am
3. 11:45 am
4. 15:15
5. 17:50
6. 15:40
7. 00:07
8. 20:48
9. 46 minutes
10. 33 minutes
11. 5:37 pm
12. 11:06 pm

Set C

1. 10:30 am
2. 8:56 am
3. 10:55 am
4.
5.
6. D
7. E
8. 08:24
9. 20:50
10. 23:49
11. 73 minutes, or 1 hour and 13 minutes
12. twenty-nine minutes to eight, or thirty-one minutes past seven
13. eleven minutes past ten
14. seventeen minutes past five

Pages 114-115: Solving Problems with Time — 1

Set A

1. 360 minutes
2. 180 seconds
3. 1 hour and 30 minutes
4. 90 minutes
5. 165 minutes
6. 335 minutes
7. 165 seconds
8. 70 minutes
9. 290 minutes
10. 360

Set B

1. 495 minutes
2. 65 minutes
3. 600 seconds
4. 120 minutes
5. 105 seconds
6. 615 seconds
7. 160 minutes
8. 140

Set C

1. 9 hours
2. 540 minutes
3. 325 minutes
4. 55 minutes
5. 600 seconds
6. 41 seconds
7. 222 seconds

Page 116: Solving Problems with Time — 2

Set A

1. 120 months
2. 114 months
3. 21 days
4. 23rd
5. 24 months
6. 42 days
7. 18 months

Set B

1. 36 months
2. 72 months
3. 56 days
4. 30th August
5. 14 days
6. 11th April
7. 84 months
8. 132 months

Set C

1. 57 days
2. 54 days
3. 71 days
4. 60 months
5. 144 months
6. 102 months
7. 13th May

Page 117: Measurement — Review 4

1. 120 seconds
2. 300 seconds
3. 90 seconds
4. 180 minutes
5. 20 minutes
6. 105 minutes
7. 21 days
8. 42 days
9. 77 days
10. 48 months
11. 84 months
12. 144 months
13. seven minutes past seven
14. thirteen minutes to eleven, or forty-seven minutes past ten
15. 10:00 am
16. 3:22 am
17. 7:48 pm
18. 11:35 pm
19. 06:00
20. 16:08
21. 00:56
22. 22:33
23. 4:20 am
24. 6:00 pm
25. 23:06
26. 15:13
27. 45 minutes
28. 34 minutes
29. 150 minutes
30. 77 minutes
31. 25 minutes
32. 54 minutes
33. Film 1: 1 hour and 5 minutes
    Film 2: 2 hours and 11 minutes
    Film 3: 2 hours and 18 minutes
34. 480 seconds
35. 175 minutes
36. 12 months
37. 120 months
38. 60 months
39. 35 days
40. 54 days

Pages 118-120: Measurement — Challenges

1. No — in foggy weather, the light can be seen up to half the distance (10 km) away. The ship is more than 10 km away from the lighthouse.
2. £278.00
3. a) i) 5 squares
      ii) 8 squares
      iii) 10 squares
   b) E.g. Method 1 — count the red squares. There are 20, so it has an area of 20 cm².
      Method 2 — multiply to find the area of the whole flag, then subtract the number of white squares: $(5 × 5) − 5 = 20$ cm².
   c) Switzerland and Italy
   d) 3 squares
4. a) Tangled Flatray: 600 g
      Grumpy Rivergup: 1000 g
      Spike-Nosed Marlin: 2000 g
      Purple Snarkfish: 400 g
   b) 2400 g
   c) 6000 g
   d) 5 (Spike-Nosed Marlins)
5. a) 250 g
   b) 10 g
6. a) 2 pumpkins
      or 2 aubergines and 4 tomatoes
      or 1 aubergine, 2 tomatoes and 1 pumpkin
   b) 1 aubergine, 1 tomato and 2 pumpkins
      or 3 aubergines and 5 tomatoes
      or 19 tomatoes
      or 2 aubergines, 3 tomatoes and 1 pumpkin
7. There are six possible answers:
   23:44, 23:48, 23:49, 23:54, 23:58, 23:59
8. a) 7 m
   b) Under the sofa
   c) Behind the coat stand
9. 4:45 pm

Section 6 — Geometry

Page 121: 2D Shapes

Set A

1. quadrilateral (square), 4 sides
2. (isosceles) triangle, 3 sides
3. pentagon, 5 sides
4. octagon, 8 sides

5. B
6. F
7. L

Set B

1-3. A: 6 sides, 6 angles, hexagon
B: 5 sides, 5 angles, pentagon
C: 3 sides, 3 angles, (isosceles) triangle
D: 4 sides, 4 angles, quadrilateral
E: 4 sides, 4 angles, quadrilateral (square)
F: 6 sides, 6 angles, hexagon
4. B, C, D, F
5. A, E

Set C

1-2. A: 6 angles, hexagon
B: 7 angles, heptagon
C: 4 angles, quadrilateral
D: 8 angles, octagon
E: 3 angles, triangle
F: 4 angles, quadrilateral
(square)

3. A, F
4. D, F — all sides
and angles equal.
5. A, B, C, E —
not all sides and
angles are equal.

Pages 122-123: Triangles

Set A

1. isosceles
2. right-angled
3. equilateral
4. scalene
5. C — A, B and D are all
isosceles, but C isn't.
6. G — it's the only
equilateral / the only one
without a right angle.

7. M — it's right-angled,
but J, K and L are all
equilateral / don't
have right angles.
8. 2 equilateral,
2 right-angled
9. 1 equilateral,
2 right-angled,
1 scalene, 3 isosceles
10. 1 isosceles,
4 right-angled

Set B

1. 1 isosceles,
2 right-angled, 3 equilateral
2. 1 isosceles, 1 equilateral,
7 right-angled
3. 1 isosceles,
1 right-angled,
1 scalene, 2 equilateral
4. equilateral

5. isosceles
6. scalene
7. right-angled
8. false
9. true
10. false

Set C

1. 3
2. 10
3. 2
4. 8
5. equilateral
6. isosceles
7. isosceles
8. scalene
9. isosceles
10. equilateral

11. True — in an isosceles
triangle with the two
equal angles at the
bottom, if a vertical line
is drawn from the top
corner to the bottom,
this will make two
right-angled triangles.
12. True — they are
isosceles because two
of the sides are the
same length. (They are
also both right-angled
triangles.)

Pages 124-125: Quadrilaterals

Set A

1. A = square,
B = trapezium,
C = rectangle,
D = parallelogram,
E = kite,
F = rhombus.
2. G, H & L. They all have
2 pairs of opposite sides the
same length and parallel, and all
of their 4 angles are right angles.

3. square
4. trapezium
5. parallelogram/rhombus
6. 24 cm
7. 13 cm
8. 18 cm

Set B

1. Trapezium. It only has one pair of parallel sides.
2. Rectangle. 4 right angles, opposite sides
(but not all sides) same length, opposite sides parallel.
3. Rhombus. 4 equal sides, opposite angles equal
(but not right angles), diagonals cross at right angles.
4. Parallelogram. Opposite sides the same length and parallel,
opposite angles equal (but not right angles).
5. Square. All sides same length, 4 right angles.
6. Kite. Two pairs of sides the same length
(but not opposite sides), one pair of opposite
angles equal, diagonals cross at right angles.
7. 4 right angles.
Accept drawing with 4 right angles and
2 pairs of opposite sides the same length.
8. 1 pair of opposite angles equal.
Accept drawing with 1 pair of opposite angles equal,
2 pairs of sides the same length (but not opposite sides)
and diagonals that cross at right angles.
9. Opposite angles equal.
Accept drawing with opposite angles equal, 4 sides
the same length and diagonals that cross at right angles.
10.

	all sides equal	not all sides equal
all angles equal	square	rectangle
not all angles equal	rhombus	parallelogram, kite, trapezium

Set C

1. Square. All sides same length, 4 right angles.
2. Quadrilateral. No special properties.
3. Trapezium. Only one pair of opposite sides parallel.
4. Quadrilateral. No special properties.
5. Rhombus. 4 equal sides, opposite angles equal (but not right angles), diagonals cross at right angles.
6. Kite. Two pairs of sides the same length, one pair of opposite angles equal, angles cross at right angles.
7. E.g. They both have 4 right angles / diagonals same length / opposite sides same length / opposite sides parallel.
8. Both have (at least) one pair of opposite sides parallel.
9. E.g. They both have two pairs of sides the same length / (at least) one pair of opposite angles equal.
10. Any two from: e.g. A square has 4 right angles, a rhombus has none. / Square diagonals are same length, rhombus diagonals differ. / A square has 4 equal angles, a rhombus only has 2 pairs of equal angles.
11. A rhombus has 4 sides same length, a parallelogram only has opposite sides same length. Rhombus diagonals cross at right angles, parallelogram diagonals do not.
12. Any two from: e.g. A parallelogram has 2 pairs of opposite angles equal, a kite has only 1 pair of opposite angles equal. / Kite diagonals cross at right angles, parallelogram diagonals do not. / A parallelogram has opposite sides parallel, a kite has no parallel sides.
13. No right angles:
    E.g.

    At least one right angle:
    E.g.

    It is not possible for a trapezium to only have one right-angle. Either none or two are needed for one pair of sides to be parallel.

Pages 126-127: Angles

Set A

1. b	5. j	9. right angle
2. c	6. l	10. acute
3. f	7. obtuse	11. obtuse
4. g	8. acute	12. acute

Set B

1. C, F, H, I, J	5. S, U, V, T	8. right angle
2. A, B, D, E, G	6. Y, X, Z, W	9. obtuse
3. N, M, L, K	7. acute	10. acute
4. P, Q, R, O		

Set C

1. c, f, h, j	5. acute	9. A
2. a, b, d, e, i	6. obtuse	10. D, E, F, G
3. f, h, j, c	7. obtuse	11. J
4. d, a, e, b, i	8. obtuse	12. M, O

Pages 128-129: Lines of Symmetry

Set A

1. three lines of symmetry
2. four lines of symmetry
3. two lines of symmetry
4. no lines of symmetry
5.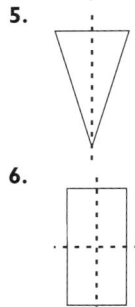
6.

7.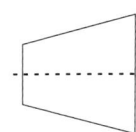
8.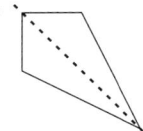
9.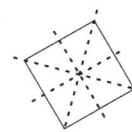
10.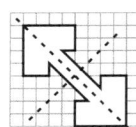
11.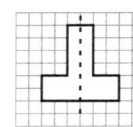
12.

Set B

1. 5
2. 3
3. None
4. 4
5. 2
6. 1
7. 4
8. 3
9. A, B, D, F

10.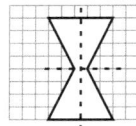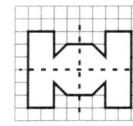

Set C

1. A, F
2. B, E
3. C
4. D
5.

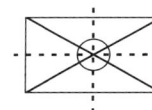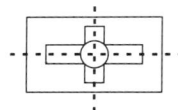

6. Each regular polygon has as many lines of symmetry as it does sides/angles:

Page 130: Geometry — Review 1

1. C, A, D, B, E
2. C
3. H
4. equilateral
5. right-angled
6. isosceles
7. scalene
8. equilateral and isosceles
9. right-angled and right-angled
10. equilateral and right-angled
11. isosceles and scalene
12. D — rectangle
13. F — rhombus
14. Opposite sides same length and parallel
15. All sides same length, opposite sides parallel
16. Opposite sides same length and parallel
17. 2 pairs of sides same length
18. All sides same length, opposite sides parallel
19. 1 pair of sides parallel
20. b, c, d, a
21. h, g, e, f
22. acute
23. right angle
24. acute
25. obtuse
26. b
27. d
28. C
29. Z
30. M

Pages 131-132: Reflection

Set A

1.
2.
3.
4.
5.
6.
7. C

Set B

1.
2.
3.
4.
5.
6.
7.
8.
9.

Set C

1.
2.
3.
4.
5.
6.
7.
8.

Page 133: Coordinates

Set A

1. Q
2. B
3. S
4. F
5. H
6. LUKE
7. MARK

Set B

1. (2, 9)
2. (4, 7)
3. The bank
4. The library (8, 7)
5. The post office (7, 3)
6. The cinema and the post office
7. The bakery and the school

Set C

1. U
2. Z = (6, 3)
3. S = (3, 4) and L = (5, 4)
4. C, U
5. G, O, T

Page 134: Translation

Set A

1. 1, 2
2. left, up

3-6.

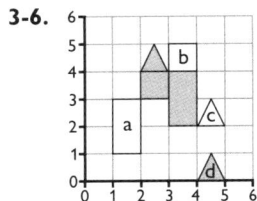

Set B

1. 2 squares right, 2 squares up.
2. 2 squares left, 3 squares down.
3. 6 squares left, 5 squares up.
4. 2 squares right, 3 squares down.

5-6.

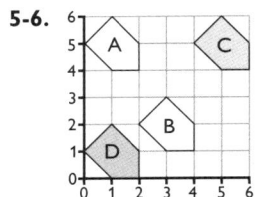

Set C

1. Green triangle =
   5 squares right,
   3 squares down.
   Red rectangle =
   2 squares right,
   5 squares up.
   Blue shape =
   3 squares left,
   1 square down

2. 3 squares left, 2 squares down.
3. 5 squares right, 1 square up.
4. 5 squares left, 1 square down.

   For example, you do the exact opposite as before.

Page 135: Plotting Points

Set A

1-9.

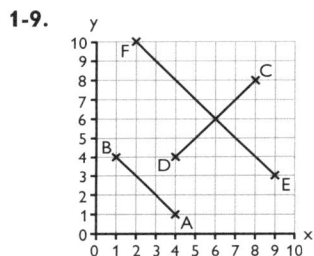

10. (6, 6)

Set B

1-9.

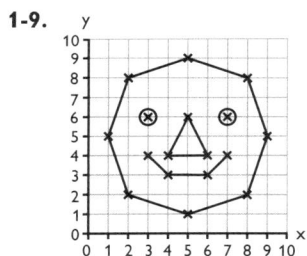

Set C

1-5.

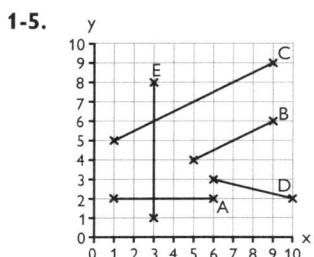

6. B and C
7. A and E
8. (3, 2)
9. (3, 6)
10. B

Page 136: Drawing Shapes

Set A

1. trapezium
2. (isosceles) triangle
3. rectangle
4. square

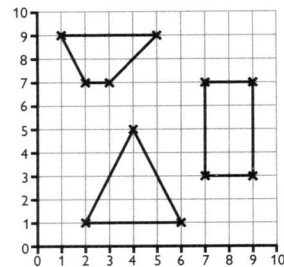

Set B

1-2.

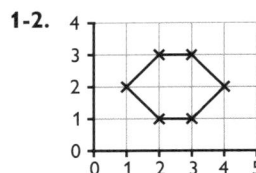

3. hexagon

4-5.

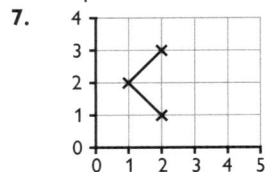

6. trapezium

7.

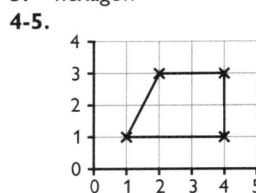

8. (3, 2)

Set C

1. (2, 3)
2. (1, 1)
3. (4, 4)
4. (4, 2)
5. For example: in Questions 1-3, there are only two different values used for the x-coordinates and two for the y-coordinates.
   In Question 4, there are four different values for both the x-coordinates and y-coordinates.
   This is because the square in Question 4 is at an angle.

6.

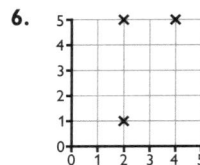

7. (4, 1)

8.

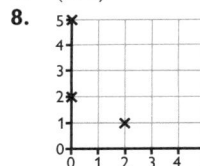

9. (2, 4)

Page 137: Geometry — Review 2

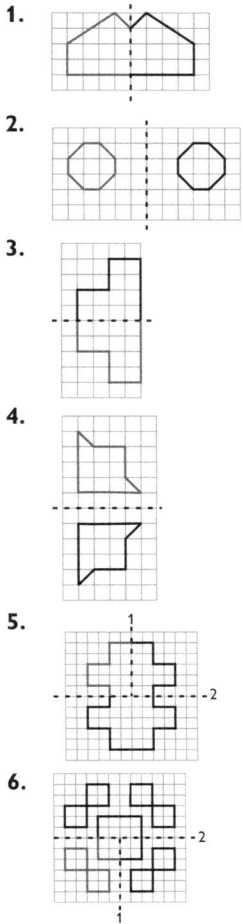

1.

2.

3.

4.

5.

6.

7. A
8. B
9. (8, 2)
10. (7, 4)

11. L
12. S and O
13. 5 squares right, 3 squares down.
14. 1 square left, 5 squares up.
15. 4 squares left, 2 squares down.
16.

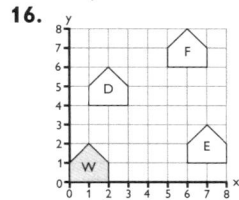

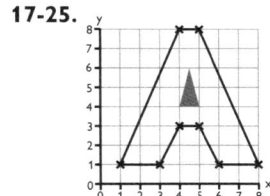

17-25.

The letter A

26.

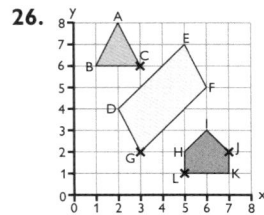

27. (isosceles) triangle
28. see above
29. parallelogram
30. see above
31. pentagon

Pages 138-140: Geometry — Challenges

1. a) 19/05/2008
   b) 27/03/1964
2. a) 90°
   b) Peak B is also obtuse. It is a scalene triangle.
   c) E, B, C, D, A
   d) She is correct. The reflected peak will be the same distance away from the 0 m/mirror line as the true peak, which is 4000 m. 4000 m + 4000 m = 8000 m
   e) 5000 m

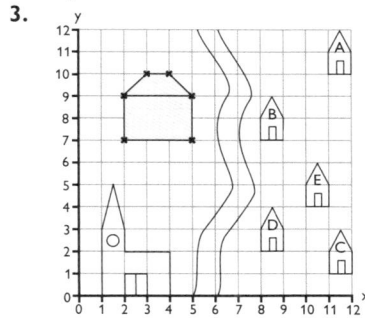

3.

4. a) The reflected patterns should appear as so:

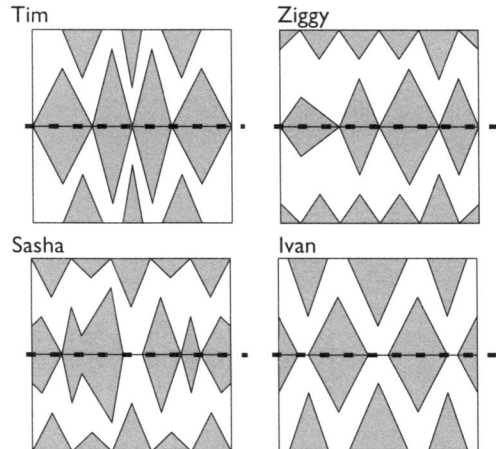

   b) Tim and Ivan have a vertical line of symmetry.

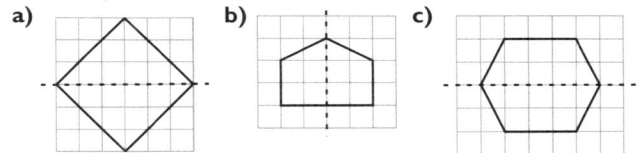

5. For example:

   Other answers are possible.

6. a) (10, 3)
   b) 8 right, 2 up
   c) (6, 7)
   d) Matilda is correct.
   e) 11 right, 13 up (or 11 east, 13 north)

Section 7 — Statistics

Pages 141-142: Tables

Set A

1. swimming
2. Aisha
3. Ben
4. Wednesday
5. Lukas
6. hockey and tennis
7. badminton
8. Thursday
9. tennis
10. *see below*
11. Saturday
12. singing
13. drumming

10.

	Friday	Saturday	Sunday
Kelechi	guitar	guitar	—
Chloe	—	singing	singing
Bartek	—	drumming	drumming
Annalea	singing	guitar	singing

Set B

1. 2015
2. Grant and Helen
3. 6
4. 8 cm
5.

Pet	Number of votes
Dog	8
Cat	4
Rabbit	12
Hamster	7
Budgie	1

6. 32
7.

	Jan	Feb	Mar
Zoomer	12	17	26
Rapid Racer	23	20	25
Overdrive	5	3	9

Set C

1. £10
2. 7
3. winter
4. Ellen
5.

	Mon	Tue	Wed	Thur	Fri
Neville	football	tennis	tennis	—	tennis
Leila	tennis	football	football	football	tennis

6.

	Week 1	Week 2	Week 3	Week 4
Vincent	5	9	6	9
Michaela	7	7	7	8
Henry	4	12	8	7

7. Week 2

Pages 143-144: Bar Charts

Set A

1-2.

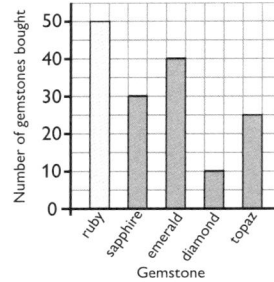

3. diamond
4. 30
5. topaz
6. ruby

7-9.

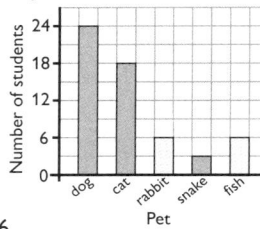

10. 6

Set B

1.

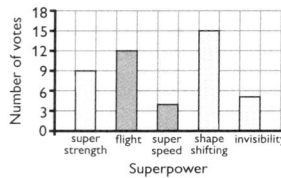

2. shape shifting
3. 9
4. super speed
5. No — flight would have 14 votes which is less than the most popular superpower (shape shifting with 15).

6.

Colour	Number of cars
green	3
red	10
yellow	5
purple	9
blue	7

7.

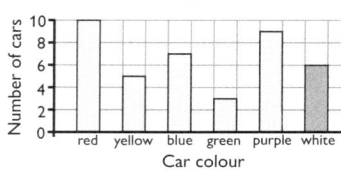

Set C

1-2.

	Number of boys	Number of girls
Year 4	10	16
Year 5	20	14

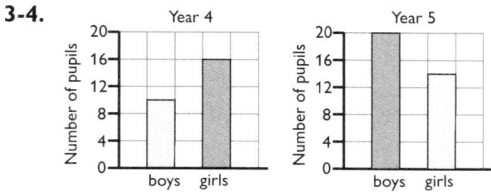

3-4.

5. see question 8
6. prickleberry
7. boomseeds — 180
8.

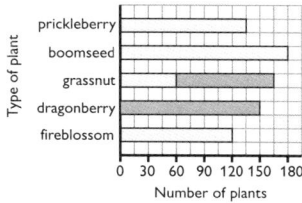

Pages 145-146: Pictograms

Set A

1. 4
2. 6
3. 3
4. Year 3
5.

6. 6
7. 5
8. Wednesday
9. Tuesday
10. 12
11. Monday
12. two and a half

Set B

1. 400
2. July
3.

4.

5. Burton — 80 mm
6. see question 9
7. Nalise
8. 75
9.

Set C

1.

2. Craig — 7
3. Olivia
4. Craig
5.

6. 2
7. May
8.

Pages 147-148: Time Graphs

Set A

1.

2. 8 miles
3. 6 miles
4. 5 minutes
5.

6. 20 cm
7. 70 cm
8. 2 months
9-11.

12. 5 °C

Set B

1. 4 seconds
2. 30 metres
3. 55 metres
4. E.g.

5. 140 litres
6. 40 litres
7. 45 seconds
8. 120 seconds

Set C

1. E.g.

2. 10 mph
3. 17.5 mph
4. Her speed was 0 mph, so she was not moving.
5. 150 cm
6. 8 am
7. 4 am, 12 pm and 4 pm
8. E.g. The tide height rose and fell twice in a similar pattern.

Page 149: Statistics — Review 1

1. Joe
2. soup
3. Neil
4-6.

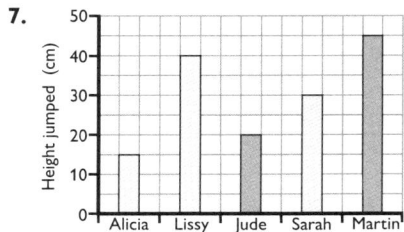

	2012	2013	2014	2015
Sally	7	6	12	10
Greg	7	10	10	10
Steph	0	0	14	10

7.

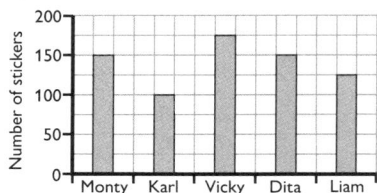

8. Lissy
9-10. E.g.

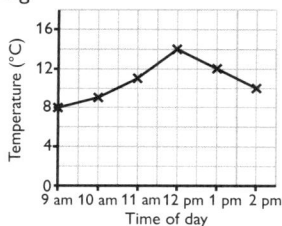

11-14.

Cardmania	♡ ♡ ♥ ◗
Paper-Cuts	♥ ♥ ♥
Cards-R-Us	♥ ◗
Card Bargains	♥ ♥

15.

Gavin	⊛ ⊛
Bella	⊛ ⊛ ⊛ ◔
Bartek	⊛ ⊛ ⊛ ◹
Rob	⊛ ◔

16. more
17. 60 m
18. 45 m
19. 45 seconds
20. E.g.

Pages 150-151: Solving Problems with Tables

Set A

1-2.

	Pupils with one brother	Pupils with one sister
Year 3	7	7
Year 4	9	4
Year 5	10	5
Year 6	6	12
Total	32	28

3. 5
4. 18
5. red
6. 31
7-8.

	Year 3	Year 4	Year 5	Year 6
Blue	14	19	8	15
Red	12	10	19	15
Total	26	29	27	30

9. 7
10. 1

Set B

1.

Fruit	Number of times eaten
apple	6
banana	3
orange	4
peach	4
pear	2

2. apple — 6
3. pear — 2

4. 200
5. 700
6. April
7. 200
8. four

Set C

1. 3
2. 3
3. 5
4. basketball
5. 125
6. Ben and Guy
7. Marcia

8. Phil
9. Ben
10. Danni's column should say 200 songs
11. 845
12. 1215 less

Pages 152-153: Solving Problems with Bar Charts

Set A

1. school A
2. 25
3. 375
4. school B
5. 875
6. 20 m
7. Mia
8. No
9. 85 m
10. 15 m
11. Area 4
12. 20
13. 60
14. Area 2
15. 165

Set B

1. Chris — 35
2. Ava
3. 110
4. 75
5. E.g.

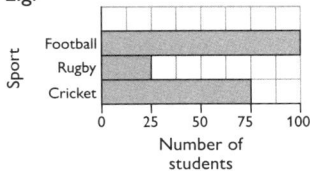

6. 75
7. 175
8. 10
9. £140

Set C

1. 125
2. 250
3. 390
4. February
5. 4 months — March, April, October and November
6. 8
7. winter

Pages 154-155: Solving Problems with Pictograms

Set A

1. quizzes
2. 15
3. 5
4. 110
5. 11
6. 5
7. 43
8. 4
9. Mal — 4
10. 7
11. 17
12. Alex, Nia, Seren, Mal
13. 35

Set B

1. 43
2. 12
3. 5
4. 25
5. Nicki
6. 450
7. Jackie
8. Ties-R-Us
9. 200
10. 1600

Set C

1. 75
2. Fabio's and Nelly's
3. 400
4. 60
5. 45
6. 300
7. 21
8. 140
9. 28
10. 70

Pages 156-157: Solving Problems with Time Graphs

Set A

1. 1 pm
2. 11 am and 3 pm
3. 8 °C
4. 4 pm
5. 100 m
6. 300 m
7. 50 cm
8. Weeks 3 and 4
9. 225 cm

Set B

1. 50 m
2. 130 seconds
3. 70 seconds
4. 12 minutes
5. 30 °C
6. September
7. 2 m
8. 4 m

Set C

1. 10 am
2. 2 °C
3. 16 °C
4. 6 minutes
5. 8 minutes
6. 40 m
7. E.g. Between 16 and 32 minutes, the kite is slowly moving down towards the ground.

Page 158: Statistics — Review 2

1.

	Iain	Rosie	Owen	Cathy
Walk	10	2	10	9
Drive	10	23	12	12
Cycle	10	5	8	9

2. Iain
3.

	Year 2	Year 3	Year 4	Year 5	Year 6
Boys	24	20	16	22	14
Girls	12	10	8	11	7
Total	36	30	24	33	21

4. 96
5. 48
6. Monday
7. Sunday
8. 12
9. C — one box can be halved to show 50.
    A and B are not suitable because it would be difficult to divide 500 or 250 to show 350 and 200 clearly.
    D is not suitable because you would have to draw lots of pictures to show the number of boxes.
10. summer
11. 900
12. 210 minutes, or 3 hours and 30 minutes
13. 120 mm
14. 60 mm
15. 60 mm
16. 11 am, 3 pm, 3:30 pm, 4 pm
17. 150 minutes

Pages 159-160: Statistics — Challenges

1. a) Picture should feature: 5 legs, 2 arms, 3 heads, 4 eyes and 6 antennae.

   b)
   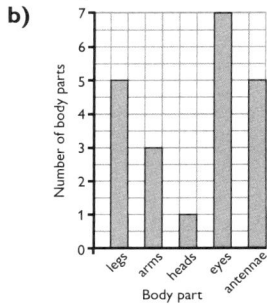

2. a) First shot
   b) Second shot
   c) Third shot

3. c) E.g. a bar chart is better for showing time in seconds. It would be difficult to show a decimal number accurately using a pictogram.

4. a) 4
   b) 20
   c) 10
   d) 660

5. a) True — the average number of bike rides in May was 16 and in April was 8.

   b) Can't say — e.g. the table shows the average number of bike rides, not how many pupils rode their bikes.

   c) Can't say — e.g. the table only shows the average for the whole month of July.

6. a) E.g.
   A — the bars are different widths and unequal spaces between each one. The bars should all be the same width with the same space between each bar.

   B — there is no key showing what each picture represents (e.g. 1 picture = 10 butterflies).

   C — the scale on the y-axis is too large, making the points hard to read. The points should be plotted on a graph with smaller numbers going up the y-axis.

   D — the numbers have no meaning. There should be a description of what the numbers show (e.g. the number of fruits picked).

   b) E.g.

   A
   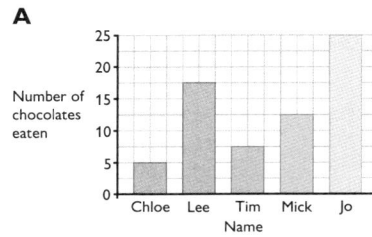

   B

   key: = 10 butterflies
   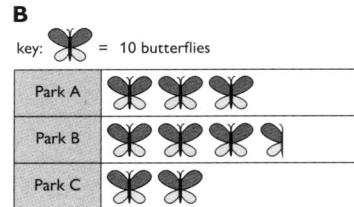

   C
   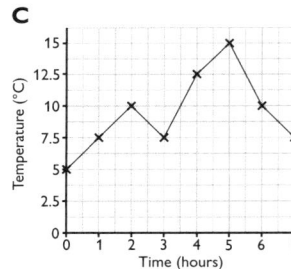

   D
   The table below shows the number of apples, pears and plums that were picked over 6 days.

	Day 1	Day 2	Day 3	Day 4	Day 5	Day 6	Total
Apples	21	19	14	7	9	12	82
Pears	10	15	15	5	15	10	70
Plums	11	9	9	8	15	12	64

M4PBA21